CHARLES
SHEELER

31 Bucks County Barn 1923

ESSAYS BY
MARTIN FRIEDMAN
BARTLETT HAYES
CHARLES MILLARD

CHARLES SHEELER

PUBLISHED FOR
THE NATIONAL COLLECTION
OF FINE ARTS
BY THE
SMITHSONIAN INSTITUTION PRESS
CITY OF WASHINGTON
1968

National Collection of Fine Arts
Smithsonian Institution
Washington, D. C.

10 October through 24 November, 1968

Philadelphia Museum of Art
Philadelphia, Pennsylvania

10 January through 16 February, 1969

Whitney Museum of American Art
New York, New York

11 March through 27 April, 1969

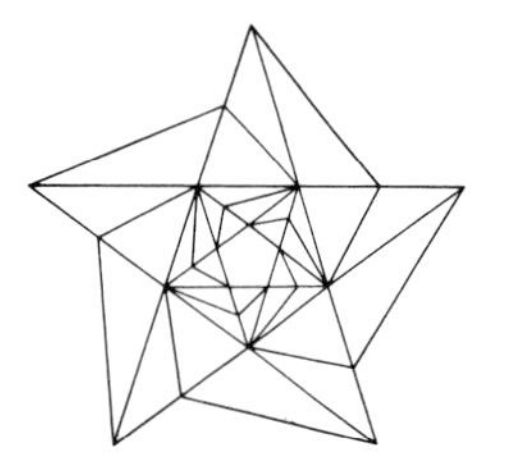

Distributed in the United States and Canada
by Random House, Inc.

Smithsonian Publication 4746

Library of Congress Catalogue 68-57069

Designed by Stephen Kraft
Printed by Vinmar Lithographing Company

CONTENTS

FOREWORD

More rapidly than we are perhaps aware,. the familiar leaders of American art of the earlier half of the century have dropped away during the 1960s. It is a time for review and reassessment, as well as for a keen look ahead.

Fortunately, the National Collection of Fine Arts has been able to enlarge its program recently to allow major retrospective as well as contemporary exhibitions. It has been, or will shortly be, actively involved in memorial reviews of a number of artists, including Stuart Davis, Edward Hopper, Alexander Archipenko, Rico Lebrun, Milton Avery, and John Marin. The present exhibition of the work of Charles Sheeler is a significant link in this chain of retrospectives.

Sheeler's achievement is well summarized in this catalogue, but I cannot forego the opportunity to pay personal tribute to the artist, whose sensitively conceived, classically ordered compositions have had a lasting effect on our perception of the American environment. He has quietly moved into the front ranks of our native masters.

The concept of presenting a comprehensive exhibition of Charles Sheeler's paintings, drawings, and photographs was formed three years ago at the time of the artist's death. The National Collection was fortunate in having the early cooperation of the Philadelphia Museum and Whitney Museum of American Art as cosponsors of the project. General organization of the exhibition was under the direction of the National Collection's curator of exhibits, Harry Lowe, who also selected the paintings and drawings exhibited. Abigail Booth, Mr. Lowe's assistant, participated in the planning and execution of the exhibition from its inception, and she contributed the biographical notes, exhibitions list, and bibliography for this catalogue.

The steps between the planning and the presenting of an exhibition are not made without the assistance of many persons. For making this exhibition possible we are indebted to staff members, colleagues, collaborators, and friends. Essential to the success of the exhibition was the interest of Mrs. Charles Sheeler; Mrs. Edith Gregor Halpert, director of the Downtown Gallery which from 1931 represented Sheeler; and William Lane—a close personal friend of the Sheelers—whose collection of American art includes the largest concentration of Sheeler's paintings, so chosen that they form, in fact, a retrospective exhibition in themselves. Special thanks also go to Lloyd Goodrich for his generous contribution of knowledge and time.

An exhibition is expanded by its catalogue. The National Collection welcomes three colleagues as contributors to this catalogue: Martin Friedman and Bartlett Hayes, directors of the Walker Art Center and Addison Gallery of American Art, respectively, and Charles Millard, until recently the director of the Washington Gallery of Modern Art. In addition to his contribution to this catalogue, Mr. Millard also chose the photographs in the exhibition. These colleagues have particular experience of Sheeler's art, and their composite commentary should prove of exceptional value.

Help in the search for the artist's works and for the history of his career has come from many sources. It is hardly possible to name all of those to whom we are indebted, and only a few may be given acknowledgment here: Mrs. Aleita Hogenson and Mrs. Shirley Harren of the National Collection of Fine Arts-National Portrait Gallery Library, whose skill and ingenuity were of invaluable assistance; Robin Bolton-Smith, whose voluntary research in New York libraries contributed to the completeness of catalogue sections; and Robert M. Doty, associate curator of the Whitney Museum of American Art, whose constructive interest in the organization of the photographic section was of assistance. To these and many others, our thanks.

Ultimately, realization of an exhibition is dependent on the cooperation of the individuals and institutions holding the works of art. Sending a work for an exhibition inevitably causes inconvenience, yet the participation by the lenders to this exhibition has been consistently enthusiastic. The help we have received has been given generously, on every side, in the spirit of tribute to the artist. It is this spirit in which the National Collection of Fine Arts joined in organizing the exhibition "Charles Sheeler."

DAVID W. SCOTT
Director
National Collection of Fine Arts

LENDERS TO THE EXHIBITION

Addison Gallery of American Art, Phillips Academy
Andover, Massachusetts

Amon Carter Museum of Western Art
Fort Worth, Texas

Mr. and Mrs. Milton K. Arenberg
Chicago, Illinois

The Art Institute of Chicago
Chicago, Illinois

The Baltimore Museum of Art
Baltimore, Maryland

Charles A. Bauer
Woodbridge, Connecticut

Bert Baum
Sellersville, Pennsylvania

Mr. and Mrs. James H. Beal
Pittsburgh, Pennsylvania

Mr. and Mrs. Leigh B. Block
Chicago, Illinois

Lawrence H. Bloedel
Williamstown, Massachusetts

Dr. and Mrs. Melvin Boigon
New York, New York

The Brooklyn Museum
Brooklyn, New York

Charles E. Buckley
St. Louis, Missouri

Butler Institute of American Art
Youngstown, Ohio

California Palace of the Legion of Honor
San Francisco, California

Mr. and Mrs. Malcolm G. Chace, Jr.
Providence, Rhode Island

Cincinnati Art Museum
Cincinnati, Ohio

The Columbus Gallery of Fine Arts
Columbus, Ohio

The Corcoran Gallery of Art
Washington, D. C.

The Currier Gallery of Art
Manchester, New Hampshire

The Detroit Institute of Arts
Detroit, Michigan

The Downtown Gallery
New York, New York

Mrs. Ernest Frederick Eidlitz
Winter Park, Florida

George Hopper Fitch
New York, New York

Fogg Art Museum, Harvard University
Cambridge, Massachusetts

Mrs. Edsel B. Ford
Grosse Pointe Shores, Michigan

Fort Worth Art Association
Fort Worth, Texas

General Motors Research Laboratories
Warren, Michigan

Mr. and Mrs. George Greenspan
New York, New York

Hallmark Cards, Inc.
Kansas City, Missouri

Mrs. Edith Gregor Halpert
New York, New York

Mr. and Mrs. Anthony Haswell
Dayton, Ohio

Bernard Heineman, Jr.
New York, New York

Mr. and Mrs. G. Gordon Hertslet
St. Louis, Missouri

Mr. and Mrs. John S. Hilson
New York, New York

Joseph H. Hirshhorn Foundation
New York, New York

Mrs. Earle Horter
Philadelphia, Pennsylvania

Illinois Institute of Technology
Chicago, Illinois

O'Donnell Iselin
New York, New York

Dr. and Mrs. Herbert J. Kayden
New York, New York

Lane Collection
Leominster, Massachusetts

William H. Lane Foundation
Leominster, Massachusetts

Library of Congress
Washington, D. C.

MacDougall Collection
Pacific Palisades, California

The Metropolitan Museum of Art
New York, New York

Mrs. Agnes E. Meyer
Washington, D. C.

Munson-Williams-Proctor Institute
Utica, New York

Museum of Art, Carnegie Institute
Pittsburgh, Pennsylvania

Museum of Art
Rhode Island School of Design
Providence, Rhode Island

Museum of Fine Arts
Boston, Massachusetts

Museum of Fine Arts
Springfield, Massachusetts

The Museum of Modern Art
New York, New York

Dr. Walter Myden
New York, New York

National Collection of Fine Arts
Smithsonian Institution
Washington, D. C.

Mr. and Mrs. Roy R. Neuberger
New York, New York

The Newark Museum
Newark, New Jersey

Carol Brandt Pavenstedt
New York, New York

Mr. and Mrs. George Perutz
Dallas, Texas

Philadelphia Museum of Art
Philadelphia, Pennsylvania

The Phillips Collection
Washington, D. C.

The Sara Roby Foundation
New York, New York

Governor and Mrs. Winthrop Rockefeller
Little Rock, Arkansas

Nathaniel Saltonstall
Boston, Massachusetts

Santa Barbara Museum of Art
Santa Barbara, California

Smith College Museum of Art
Northampton, Massachusetts

Mrs. Otto L. Spaeth
New York, New York

Mrs. Edward Steichen
West Redding, Connecticut

Stephen and Sybil Stone Foundation
Newton Centre, Massachusetts

Mr. and Mrs. Robert D. Straus
Houston, Texas

Mr. and Mrs. Karl Swenson
Beverly Hills, California

The Toledo Museum of Art
Toledo, Ohio

Mrs. Edwin Litchfield Turnbull
Houston, Texas

Virginia Museum of Fine Arts
Richmond, Virginia

Walker Art Center
Minneapolis, Minnesota

Whitney Museum of American Art
New York, New York

Wichita Art Museum
Wichita, Kansas

Anne Burnett Windfohr
Fort Worth, Texas

Yale University Art Gallery
New Haven, Connecticut

INTRODUCTION TO THE EXHIBITION

There is nothing obscure about Charles Sheeler—in either the sense of personal fame or the sense of communication. Few of our native artists are so well and amply documented or have been so often and widely exhibited. Since his first show, 60 years ago, this is the 40th exhibition to feature his work. This statistic, of course, does not discriminate between exposures of a handful of works and the major retrospective organized by the Museum of Modern Art in 1939, the Art Galleries of the University of California at Los Angeles in 1954, and the University of Iowa in 1963, but it indicates that Sheeler did not lack for professional recognition. He also enjoyed the warmth of popular and critical response to his work. Certainly a large part of the responsibility for this continuous rapport between his art and its audience is his early commitment to an artistic credo and faithful adherence to it. For demonstration, one may cite Forbes Watson's article on him of 1923, the first significant critical appraisal on Sheeler published, which is as valid today as it was when written.

As an artist it is not so remarkable that Sheeler's paintings were based on consistent aesthetic convictions. What is unusual is that the vocabulary of forms which he developed, refined, and expanded in a strong, straight line from these convictions communicated broadly and with clarity of diction. Sheeler was and continues to be popular, yet he never contrived to fashion. Perhaps the explanation is found in Sheeler's own belief that honest art was an organic growth of its immediate time and cultural history. Sheeler's gift was that with a clear perception of how this "rule" applied to himself, he participated in creating the form of 20th-century American art and conformed to the spirit and cultural history of his country. Thus he produced an art which may be at once respected and loved.

For all the attention Sheeler and his art have received, there persists a sense that the accumulation of knowledge of him is fragmented. Perhaps this is because he was always within such easy reach. Primarily, then, this exhibition and publication are an opportunity to offer material for a composite review of Sheeler with the objectivity gained from a distance in time—three years from his death and nine years from the cruelly abrupt cessation of his activity as an artist caused by a paralytic stroke.

Recognizing the opportunity to make a conclusive evaluation presented by sponsorship of this exhibition, it was early determined that the visual evidence of his career must be produced in quantity, and that many works not seen since the time of their execution should be brought again into public view. The exhibition quite intentionally became the largest assembly of Sheeler works.

The responsibility of decision on individual works to be invited for the exhibit was shared with Miss Abigail Booth. Almost as soon as we set about a review of the total Sheeler *oeuvre* his reputation for consistency of statement was unmistakably proven. Another basic characteristic of his work was also clearly recognized from this exercise in overview: the recurrence of a very few subject motifs. That Sheeler expressed his conceptual statement in a small vocabulary of forms is not a discovery. It is implied in critics' repeated references to "his barns," "his interiors"—the serial character recognized in much of his production. Sheeler's basic intention was to distill a single expression of the visual order and coherency in real objects, not to present a relatively realistic rendering of environment. The few subjects which served his purpose and the stylistic unity in them at any given period in time, to us, demonstrated this point.

Categorizing the art objects according to themes as a device for comparison and selection was the immediate application of the principle. There was a simultaneous realization that attention could be drawn to the integrity of his artistic viewpoint through identification with subject themes; this was a valid way both to present a review of his work and to induce a fresh viewpoint of his total production. The standard exhibition contents record is, therefore, presented in a form which serves as a schematic description of his artistic directions and his life. The columnar organization of the catalogue listings—vertically by thematic concern and horizontally by date—may seem to be a coercion of a creative imagination. This parallel ordering was made to be read not as a segregation of disparate aspects of Sheeler's work but as a graphic demonstration of the unity of his art.

The exhibition was planned to bring together a maximum of the artist's work and thereby offer material for a composite view of his achievement. The same intention underlies the structure of this publication. The juxtaposition of catalogue entries with each other and with a biographical sketch is one outcome of this idea; the invitation to three critic-historians to contribute essays on the artist is another.

The exhibition titled *The Precisionist View in American Art*, given by the Walker Art Center of Minneapolis in 1960, examined a group of 16 artists allied by their visual interpretation of environment. Sheeler was one of the dominant figures in this exhibition. Martin Friedman, now director of the Walker Art Center, was the initiator of that exhibit and author of its catalogue essay, which was an outstanding analysis of a major trend in American painting of the 20th century. There Mr. Friedman made a perceptive statement on Charles Sheeler in the context of a group of artists linked by relationships of style and intention. Clearly, he had more to say and more that was well worth hearing, given the opportunity to concentrate on Sheeler alone. We are fortunate that Mr. Friedman agreed that this exhibition publication was a suitable opportunity. He has provided us with the thorough and objective examination of the artist's development, achievement, and place in the pattern of American painting.

Bartlett Hayes has long been a personal friend of the artist and his wife. An outstanding teacher and scholar of 20th-century American art, he is credited with starting the first artist-in-residence program at an academic institution. The artist he invited to initiate this program in 1946 at Phillips Academy, Andover, was Charles Sheeler. From this experience a personal acquaintance grew into a warm and lasting friendship between the two families. The influence of the residency on Sheeler was the realization of the imagery that would dominate his last decade of painting. Mr. Hayes is uniquely qualified to tell of the experience of Sheeler's visit at Andover, its impact on the direction of his work, and of the man himself. He was invited to add the component to this publication that would be both a friend's and scholar's commentary. We are fortunate that Mr. Hayes, too, felt this was the appropriate time and place to articulate his special understanding of the artist.

Charles Sheeler is acknowledged as one of the finest American painters of our century; it is often forgotten or unknown that he was equally an artist with a camera. For many years, a common distortion of the relationship of photography and "art" has cast suspicion on the practice of photography by painters. (Sheeler himself was clear and outspoken on the distinct merits of each medium and held both in respect.) The intellectual prejudice against the camera is fast dying, but it contributes to a suppression of this important aspect of Sheeler's creativity. A symptom of this recognition of the camera as a legitimate artistic medium is the background Charles Millard brings to his essay in this catalogue. An art historian with a trained eye on both the art of the ancient and the most modern worlds, Mr. Millard also has devoted special study to the art of photography. Charles Sheeler has particularly drawn his attention. The stylistic independence and artistic sensitivity Sheeler showed in the photography medium clearly warrants this attention. Mr. Millard's breadth of understanding makes him singularly qualified to contribute the third part of a composition on the art of Charles Sheeler.

The exhibition was designed to offer substantial evidence of an artist's accomplishment; the catalogue was designed to present several critical appraisals of that accomplishment and provide documentation for independent analysis. Those of us who have participated in the production of both have acquired a deeper and more informed respect for Charles Sheeler's refined and disciplined vision. It is our hope that our efforts communicate with something of the clarity that was Charles Sheeler's.

HARRY LOWE
Curator of Exhibits
National Collection of Fine Arts

CATALOGUE OF THE EXHIBITION AND BIOGRAPHICAL NOTES

Catalogue numbers in bold face
Dimensions are in inches; height precedes width.
All photographs exhibited are lent anonymously.

1883 Charles R. Sheeler, Junior, born in Philadelphia 16 July.

His upbringing was conventional with the possible exception that by the time he was 17 he had decided that, more than anything else, he wanted to paint. With parental sanction, he sought professional guidance on how to prepare for his objective. The advice received was pessimistic: if he expected to support himself through the practice of art, he would be wiser to study its useful employment.

1900-1903 Therefore, immediately upon completing secondary school he entered Philadelphia's School of Industrial Art for the three-year general course. He worked principally in applied design, learning historical orders of ornament to be made into commonplace patterns for commonplace decoration. The training might have provided future security but it did not satisfy. At the end of the three years Sheeler still wanted to paint more than anything else.

1903-1906 Entirely confident of his creative intention, Sheeler entered the Pennsylvania Academy of the Fine Arts. He enrolled in the still life and life classes of William Merritt Chase; in spring there was sketching in the country around Philadelphia. Chase was an accomplished and successful artist, and entrancing teacher. The emphasis of the study was attainment of the Chase manner, an eminently desirable goal at the time. The successful painter captured a fleeting glimpse of scenery with an attractive and obvious display of technique. Spontaneity of brushwork and expression was the artist's measure. Display of the subject and of the dexterity in its rendering was the function of the painting. Sheeler, with both skill and allegiance to this canon, was an outstanding student.

Optional adjuncts to the course were Chase-conducted summer excursions to Europe, where the students were introduced to the approved old masters, especially Hals and Velasquez, in the museums and to later masters, such as John Sargent, Edwin Abbey, Sir Lawrence Alma-Tadema, in their studios. Sheeler's first experiences of Europe, its artists, and its museums were with the Chase tour of 1904 to London and Holland and the tour of 1905 to Spain.

He spent the summer of 1906 in a less exotic environment—Gloucester, Massachusetts. Now a graduate artist with six years of training behind him—three in the tedious exercise of simple manual skill and three in the exciting exercise of inventive image-making—Sheeler adhered to Chase's style in all things.

With the fall, Sheeler settled into the work of a professional painter. Contented within the standards of the academy days, he produced landscapes and still lifes, varied by romantic, night-shadowed scenes involving figures. For reasons of practical economy as well as friendship, a studio cooperation was arranged between Sheeler and Morton Schamberg, a fellow Philadelphian who had studied architecture at the University of Pennsylvania before gravitating to the Chase class at the Academy. Although Schamberg was quicker to become dissatisfied with the Academy art theory than was Sheeler, an aesthetic and personal bond of unusual strength formed between them.

The year 1906 also brought Sheeler his first meager but significant mark of professional attainment: inclusion in the National Academy of Design winter exhibition. His painting was bought out of the show.

1907-1908 Sheeler continued in the conventional pattern of seeking to establish a career: painting, submitting his work for exhibition, and hoping for sales. The assistance of his parents, which carried him through this inevitably lean period, also continued, as did Schamberg's friendship and the shared studio arrangement. Sheeler was represented in the National Academy and Pennsylvania Academy of the Fine Arts annual exhibitions in both years. In 1908 a few paintings were accepted by New York dealer William Macbeth, and in November of the same year a Philadelphia gallery gave him his first one-man exhibition. Progress was slow but real.

Sheeler's parents invited Charles to accompany them on a trip to Europe, and the family sailed for Italy, December 4, 1908. They visited Naples, Rome, Venice, Milan, and Florence in December. Schamberg, who had gone alone to Paris somewhat earlier, joined them in Italy. The two young men saw the great achievements of the Italian Renaissance for the first time; Piero della Francesca made a special impression. Here were paintings in which an abstract architectonic order was imposed on visual reality—arbitrary design took precedence over representation of time and place.

1909

They spent the whole of January and part of February in Paris, and they were in London for a few days before returning to America. From experience of the 15th century's structural aesthetic, Sheeler jumped to the 20th century's most progressive renewal of it. He was introduced to the work of Cezanne, Matisse, Picasso, Bracque; analytic Cubism was just then being defined in form. The experience was brief in time and concentration, but it was absolutely decisive. The Chase way was no longer creditable.

Sheeler's reaction was profound but not abrupt—the first demonstration of a lifelong characteristic of behavior. Not slow to recognize a new impulse in his thinking, he would spend a long and deliberate time analyzing and absorbing its implications to his art. The process was largely cerebral. Little of his changing direction surfaced in paintings until an idea was near full realization in terms of design. Sheeler described the ten years following his Italian and Paris experience as a "bailing out" of the Chase indoctrination.

When I came back I couldn't resume where I had left off. I had to bail out, as I've called it before, for about ten years before I really got started on a new direction. There was no more possible justice of the model or to go out and paint a landscape. I had to plan ahead of time what ingredients a painting would have in it that would be to my satisfaction as nearly as I could arrive at them. The period of about ten years was neither fish nor fowl. It was sort of like the tadpole that still hasn't its two hind legs. He has the front ones but the tail is still on.

Philadelphia
September 26th, 1910

My Dear Mr. Macbeth,

I found your note awaiting me on my return to town last Wednesday—the pictures I received Saturday.

I was surprised and sorry that you failed to recognize the merits of my pictures. It is not possible to continue to repeat the things one has done—there must always be the elimination of the unessentials and the striving after greater qualities and to more forcefully present the essentials—or stagnation must result.

You say you hope it is only an experiment—everyone who is sincerely trying to solve the enormous difficulties of artistic expression is an experimenter and remains so as long as he is "artistically alive."

I regret that you do not care to show my pictures at this time.

Very truly yours,
C. R. Sheeler, Jr.
1626 Chestnut Street

Suspended Forms: still life | **Sun, Rocks, and Trees: landscape**

1910-1911

Back in Philadelphia after the decisive experience of Italian and French art, Sheeler's life pattern continued as before: work in the downtown studio—the orderly pursuit of painting and a career as a painter. Even choice of subjects remained much the same, only his determination of their form began to alter. Sheeler and Schamberg took a house near Doylestown in Bucks County for sketching weekends. The result, aside from the pleasures of escape to the country, was a new subject theme. As usual, there was a time gap before the visual experience would be evidenced in paintings.

Suspended Forms: still life

1 Plums on a Plate circa 1910
oil on panel 10⅛ x 13¾
Lent by The Downtown Gallery

Sun, Rocks, and Trees: landscape

2 Landscape with Waterfall 1911
oil on canvas 14⅛ x 12⅛
Lent by Bert Baum

1912

The desire for a more reliable income caused Sheeler to look about for an auxiliary vocation. He and Schamberg were companions in this as in other broad features of their lives. They both took up commercial photography. For Sheeler, the selection of photography as a means to establish an income was made on the assumption that it would be neither a drain nor an intrusion on his primary activity as creative artist. The use of the camera as a tool of expression was not a consideration, and during his first two years as a photographer he confined himself to executing assignments from Philadelphia architects to record their projects.

Suspended Forms: still life

3 Chrysanthemums 1912
oil on canvas 24 x 20
Lent by Whitney Museum of American Art

4 Dahlias and Asters 1912
oil on canvas 20⅛ x 14⅛
Lent by The Corcoran Gallery of Art, Gift of Mrs. F. H. Detweiler

5 The Mandarin 1912
oil on canvas 10⅛ x 13¾
Lent by Munson-Williams-Proctor Institute

6 Still Life, Spanish Shawl 1912
oil on canvas 10 x 14
Lent by Lane Collection

1913

Philadelphia to Manhattan is a short trip, and Sheeler made it often. He kept himself acquainted with the personalities and gallery centers of contemporary American art in New York. Arthur B. Davis had seen a few of his drawings and offered an invitation to participate in the Armory Show. [Five of the six paintings he exhibited are included in this exhibition: nos. 2, 3, 4, 5, and 7.] The show itself made a greater impression on Sheeler than his paintings made on a general audience. The European experience of 1909 was reinforced; he struck out more boldly into formal abstraction.

Sun, Rocks, and Trees: landscape

7 Landscape 1913
oil on panel 10¼ x 13¾
Lent anonymously

1915-1917

Besides paintings which in experimental variety demonstrate the "bailing out" was in progress, these years were marked by increased involvement in the New York art scene. Participation in the several group exhibitions now considered historic landmarks of 20th century American art, the Forum and Society of Independents exhibitions, led to some sales. Important friendships were formed with the Mexican artist-turned-dealer, Marius De Zayas, and with the Walter Arensbergs. There was a shift in attitude toward the use of the camera. A series on the Doylestown house, photographs taken as an expressive end in themselves, were material for a one-man exhibition in 1917 given by De Zayas at his Modern Gallery. Photography commissions changed from records for architects to records for art collectors.

Suspended Forms: still life

8 Zinnia and Nasturtium Leaves 1915
photograph

Sun, Rocks, and Trees: landscape

9 House with Trees 1915
oil on panel 10¼ x 13⅞
Lent by Museum of Art, Rhode Island School of Design

10 Landscape 1915
oil on panel 10½ x 14
Lent by Lane Collection

13 Lhasa 1916
oil on canvas 25½ x 31¾
Lent by The Columbus Gallery of Fine Arts, Ferdinand Howald Collection

American Interior: interiors

11 Stairwell 1915
photograph

On the Theme of Farm Buildings: barns

12 Pennsylvania Barn 1915
photograph

Skyline: city buildings

Industrial Architecture: factories and machines

Variations from the Themes

Suspended Forms: still life

Sun, Rocks, and Trees: landscape

14 Flower Forms 1917
oil on canvas 23¼ x 19¼
Lent by Mrs. Earle Horter

1918 Sheeler's photographic activity expanded. A Doylestown interior and a barn study took first and fourth prizes in Wanamaker's annual exhibition, where other prizes went to Schamberg and Paul Strand. Sheeler was an acknowledged professional in two media: painting and photography.

The range of his friendships and involvement in the art scene also enlarged. Arensberg, a poet and astute patron of the arts, became an especial friend. The Arensberg home was a rare American manifestation of the *salon*. Sheeler was a member of this unstructured club of intellectuals until the Arensbergs, finding the crowds pressed too hard upon their privacy, escaped in the early 20s to residence in California. It was through the Arensbergs that Sheeler came to know Marcel Duchamp and became acquainted with other Parisian emigrés. His lifelong friendship with William Carlos Williams also started at this time.

The event of 1918 which overshadows all the rest was the sudden death of Morton Schamberg. In three October days, one of America's most promising talents became a statistic of the Spanish influenza epidemic.

18 Flower in Bowl 1918
watercolor and gouache
14⅝ x 11⅝
Lent by The Columbus Gallery of Fine Arts, Ferdinand Howald Collection

1919 The shift of Sheeler's attention from Philadelphia to New York became complete when he moved to the city early in the year. The decision was precipitated by the loss of Schamberg, although the idea had long been growing in favor. He kept the Doylestown house until 1923, but visits there were increasingly less frequent.

1920-1922 De Zayas' second gallery venture opened in 1920, and shortly afterward Sheeler became a staff member. The presence of the city stimulated Sheeler to introduce another formal interest to his artistic vocabulary. With Paul Strand he made a six-minute film study of its buildings, *Manhatta,* which was first shown in July 1921 under the title *New York the Magnificent.* Inevitably, still photography of skyscrapers was a consuming interest. Visual concerns first demonstrated in photography often took several years to be assimilated and transformed by Sheeler's painter's eye into imaginatively designed canvasses. By Sheeler's judgment his struggle to become independent from Chase's discipline was completed about the time of the move to New York. The constant surroundings of the city must have been singularly congenial to the first resolution of Sheeler's intention to create paintings in terms of their structural essentials.

26 Still Life circa 1922
watercolor and charcoal 19 x 15
Lent by Mr. and Mrs. G. Gordon Hertslet

American Interior: interiors

20 Hallway 1919
oil on canvas 23¾ x 15⅞
Lent by Mrs. Edwin Litchfield Turnbull

On the Theme of Farm Buildings: barns

15 Barn Abstraction 1917
conté crayon 14⅛ x 19½
Lent by Philadelphia Museum of Art, The Louise and Walter Arensberg Collection

19 Bucks County Barn 1918
watercolor and gouache 17 x 22½
Lent by The Columbus Gallery of Fine Arts, Ferdinand Howald Collection

Skyline: city buildings

21 New York 1920
photograph

22 New York 1920
photograph

23 New York 1920
pencil 19⅞ x 13
Lent by The Art Institute of Chicago

24 Church Street El 1920
oil on canvas 16⅛ x 19⅛
Lent by Mrs. Earle Horter

25 New York circa 1920
photograph

27 Offices 1922
oil on canvas 20 x 13
Lent by The Phillips Collection

Industrial Architecture: factories and machines

Variations from the Themes

16 African Mask 1917
photograph

17 African Figures 1917
photograph

28 Pertaining to Yachts and Yachting 1922
oil on canvas 20 x 24
Lent by Philadelphia Museum of Art, Bequest of Margaretta S. Hinchman

1923 The year was one of incident for Sheeler: his first marriage; the De Zayas Gallery, never a financial success, closed that spring; through the suggestion of Edward Steichen he became a photographer for Condé Nast, working on the publications *Vogue* and *Vanity Fair,* and he began doing free-lance photography for several advertising agencies; the first of his two published pieces of art criticism appeared in *The Arts* magazine and its editor, Forbes Watson, wrote a lengthy evaluation of Sheeler's accomplishment for the same issue; and, after having exhibited regularly since 1913 in rather fraternal contexts, this year his paintings and photographs appeared in at least four objectively selected shows. Sheeler, at 40, had achieved recognition as an artist.

1924-1926 Sheeler continued to live in New York and work steadily at photography—on a commercial schedule—and at painting in what time was left. The symptomatic pattern of a successful painter began to develop: several exhibitions each year—occasionally one-man shows, more frequently participation in invitational shows surveying contemporary American art. Sheeler's inclusion in the major survey exhibits sponsored annually or biennially by several American museums would not be routine, however, until the 30s. [A listing of Sheeler's exhibitions appears elsewhere in this catalogue.] His involvement in the broader activities of the art community was necessarily diminished by the pressures of work, but his sense of being part of that community persisted. In March 1924 Sheeler organized an exhibition of work by Picasso, Braque, Duchamp, and De Zayas for the Whitney Studio Club which showed concurrently with an exhibit of his own work at the Whitney Studio Galleries.

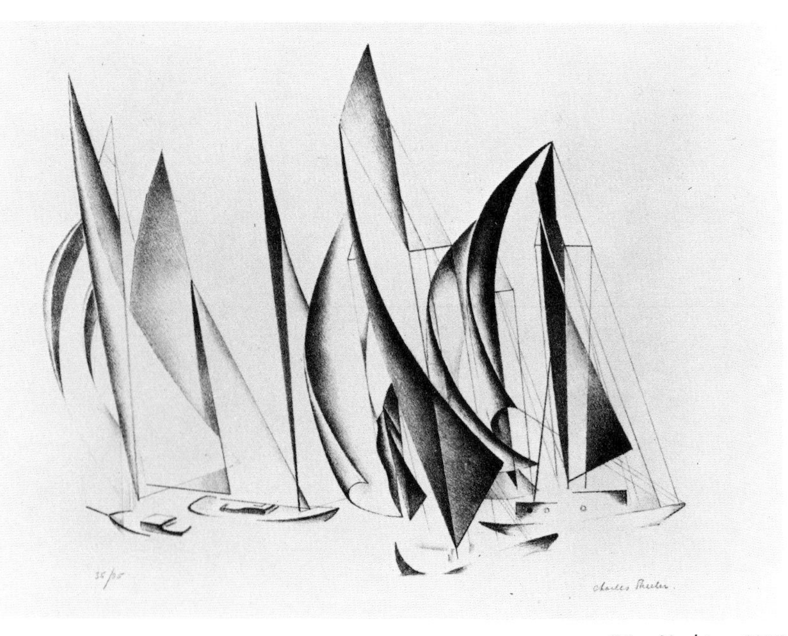

38 Yachts 1924

Suspended Forms: still life

29 Geraniums, Pots, Spaces 1923
pastel 24¼ x 19½
Lent by The Art Institute of Chicago

30 Still Life with Peaches 1923
pastel 15¾ x 11½
Lent by The Columbus Gallery of Fine Arts, Ferdinand Howald Collection

33 Objects on a Table 1924
watercolor 31 x 21
Lent by The Columbus Gallery of Fine Arts, Ferdinand Howald Collection

34 Apples 1924
color crayon 8 x 11½
Lent by Lane Collection

35 Timothy 1924
color crayon and pencil
32⅛ x 21½
Lent by Santa Barbara Museum of Art, Gift of Wright Ludington

39 Gladioli in White Pitcher 1925
oil on canvas 28½ x 22⅛
Lent by Santa Barbara Museum of Art, Gift of Wright Ludington

40 Still Life 1925
oil on canvas 24 x 20
Lent by California Palace of the Legion of Honor, Gift of Max L. Rosenberg

44 Geranium circa 1926
oil on canvas 32 x 26
Lent by Whitney Museum of American Art

Sun, Rocks, and Trees: landscape

41 Landscape—Truro 1925
tempera 4½ x 6¼
Lent by Lane Collection

42 Pennsylvania Landscape 1925
oil on canvas 10⅛ x 12⅛
Lent by Philadelphia Museum of Art, The Louis E. Stern Collection

American Interior: interiors

36 Stairway to Studio 1924
tempera, conté crayon, and pencil 25½ x 20
Lent by Mrs. Earle Horter
(exhibited in Philadelphia only)

43 Staircase, Doylestown 1925
oil on canvas 24 x 20
Lent by Joseph H. Hirshhorn Foundation

45 Interior 1926
oil on canvas 33 x 22
Lent by Whitney Museum of American Art

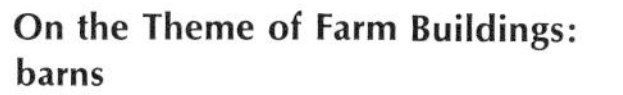

On the Theme of Farm Buildings: barns

31 Bucks County Barn 1923
tempera and crayon 19¼ x 25½
Lent by Whitney Museum of American Art

Skyline: city buildings

Industrial Architecture: factories and machines

Variations from the Themes

32 Self Portrait 1923
conté crayon, watercolor and pencil 19¾ x 25¾
Lent by The Museum of Modern Art, Gift of Abby Aldrich Rockefeller
(exhibited in New York only)

37 Self Portrait 1924
pastel 23 x 18¾
Lent by The Downtown Gallery

38 Yachts 1924
lithograph 8¼ x 10¼
Lent by National Collection of Fine Arts, Smithsonian Institution

46 Portrait circa 1926
photograph

37 Self Portrait 1924

		Suspended Forms: still life	Sun, Rocks, and Trees: landscape
1927-1928	Sheeler left New York in 1927 for the town of South Salem, New York. He spent six weeks of 1927 in Detroit on commission making a photographic record of the Ford Motor Company's River Rouge Plant. The 32 photographs which were the result brought him international fame as a photographer. The experience introduced another theme into his paintings. Sheeler is typically recognized as the artist of machine-age America, and in many respects Sheeler, too, felt the structures of modern technology were his most expressive artistic language. It is signficant, however, that his preoccupation with the architecture and artifacts of the Shaker communities dates from the same years as his first intense experience of industrial America. At base, his sense of affinity for both the early and late manufactures was the same: their functionally determined form, craftsmanship, and spiritual relevance to their special societies.	**47** Spring Interior 1927 oil on canvas 30 x 25 Lent by Lane Collection	
1929	In spring Sheeler made his fourth and last trip abroad. Planned as a vacation, the itinerary was fixed by two objectives: a long-desired visit to Chartres cathedral and the opening in Stuttgart of the exhibition *Film und Foto* in which he and many American photographers were represented. There was time for a visit to Paris and travel through Germany. The Northern Gothic paintings in German museums especially drew his attention—the meticulous realism of van Eyck, Memling, and Holbein. *Upper Deck* [no. 54], the single work most identified with Sheeler, was executed just before leaving on this trip. It broke a two-year abstinence from oil paints which began after *Spring Interior* [no. 47]: *This picture [Upper Deck] presented a marked change from Spring Interior which preceded it with an interval of two years. Spring Interior . . . [is] loosely woven in . . . execution. It was painted in the course of three or four sittings, without preliminary planning. . . . Upper Deck marked the beginning of a procedure which has continued in effect. . . . With this painting it became my custom to build up gradually a mental image of the picture before the actual work of putting it down began. Something seen which keeps reoccurring in one's memory, with insistence increasingly vivid, and with attributes added which had escaped observation on first acquaintance. In the course of time the accumulation takes on a personal identity and the picture attains a mental existence complete within the limits of one's potentiality.*		

American Interior: interiors

On the Theme of Farm Buildings: barns

Skyline: city buildings

48 Delmonico Building 1927
lithograph 9¾ x 6¾
Lent by Library of Congress

Industrial Architecture: factories and machines

49 River Rouge Plant—Power House 1927
photograph

50 River Rouge Plant—Slag Buggy 1927
photograph

51 River Rouge Plant—Stamping Press 1927
photograph

52 Funnel 1927
photograph

53 Rouge River Industrial Plant 1928
watercolor 8 x 11¼
Lent by Museum of Art, Carnegie Institute

54 Upper Deck 1929
oil on canvas 29⅛ x 22⅛
Lent by Fogg Art Museum, Harvard University, Louise E. Bettens Fund

59 American Landscape 1930
oil on canvas 24 x 31
Lent by The Museum of Modern Art, Gift of Abby Aldrich Rockefeller, 1934

Variations from the Themes

55 Chartres Cathedral 1929
photograph

56 Chartres Cathedral 1929
photograph

57 Chartres Cathedral 1929
photograph

58 Chartres Cathedral 1929
photograph

1931-1933

The breakthrough Sheeler felt he had attained in *Upper Deck* showed its effect in the quantity and character of his paintings in the early 30s. The nature of Sheeler's procedure and technique automatically limited his production—but, then, he was not by nature an impatient man.

Sheeler became associated with the Downtown Gallery in 1931. For the first time he had the representation of a dealer.

The year 1932 was the last in which he did advertising photography. The work for Condé Nast had ceased shortly before. Sheeler now used photography very little as an independent expressive medium. This year he changed his residence for the third time, moving from South Salem to Ridgefield, Connecticut. It was in June 1933 in Ridgefield that his first wife, Katherine Shaffer Sheeler, died.

1935

Late in the year, Sheeler traveled to Colonial Williamsburg to take up residence in one of the restoration's buildings until the early spring of 1936. He had a predetermined purpose: the making of photographs and subsequent execution of paintings of several of the buildings. The work was not done on formal commission, although two paintings of their major buildings are now held at Colonial Williamsburg, but it was a prototype of Sheeler's habitual working pattern in later years.

Suspended Forms: still life

60 Cactus 1931
oil on canvas 45⅛ x 30
Lent by Philadelphia Museum of Art, The Louise and Walter Arensberg Collection

70 Of Domestic Utility 1933
conté crayon 25 x 19⅜
Lent by The Museum of Modern Art, Gift of Abby Aldrich Rockefeller
(exhibited in New York only)

71 Feline Felicity 1934
conté crayon sight: 14⅛ x 13¼
Lent by Fogg Art Museum, Harvard University, Louise E. Bettens Fund

76 Coleus 1935
photograph

Sun, Rocks, and Trees: landscape

65 View of Central Park 1932
conté crayon 17¾ x 19
Lent by Governor and Mrs. Winthrop Rockefeller

American Interior: interiors

61 Home Sweet Home 1931
oil on canvas 36 x 29
Lent by The Detroit Institute of Arts, Gift of Robert H. Tannahill

62 View of New York 1931
oil on canvas 47¾ x 36¼
Lent by Museum of Fine Arts, Boston, Charles Henry Hayden Fund

66 New Haven 1932
oil on canvas 36 x 29
Lent by Lane Collection

67 Interior with Stove 1932
conté cryon 28½ x 20½
Lent by Mrs. Edward Steichen

68 Interior, Bucks County Barn 1932
conté crayon 15 x 18¾
Lent by Whitney Museum of American Art

72 American Interior 1934
oil on canvas 32½ x 30
Lent by Yale University Art Gallery, Gift of Mrs. Paul Moore

77 Stairway 1935
photograph

78 Shaker Window circa 1935
photograph

On the Theme of Farm Buildings: barns

69 Bucks County Barn 1932
oil on panel 23⅞ x 29⅞
Lent by The Museum of Modern Art, Gift of Abby Aldrich Rockefeller, 1935

73 Ephrata 1934
oil on panel 19½ x 23½
Lent by Museum of Fine Arts, Springfield

74 Shaker Buildings 1934
oil on canvas 9⅞ x 13⅞
Lent anonymously

75 Connecticut Barn and Landscape 1934
watercolor sight: 3½ x 4¾
Lent by O'Donnell Iselin

Skyline: city buildings

Industrial Architecture: factories and machines

63 Classic Landscape 1931
oil on canvas 25 x 32¼
Lent by Mrs. Edsel B. Ford

64 Ballet Mechanique 1931
conté crayon sight: 10¼ x 10
Lent by O'Donnell Iselin

79 Totems in Steel 1935
tempera sight: 3⅝ x 5
Lent by O'Donnell Iselin

80 Totems in Steel 1935
conté crayon 19⅛ x 22¾
Lent by Fogg Art Museum, Harvard University, Bequest of Meta and Paul J. Sachs

81 City Interior #2 1935
tempera 7 x 9½
Lent by Lane Collection

Variations from the Themes

1937-1939

On the suggestion of Harcourt, Brace and Company, publishers, Sheeler had written an autobiography (from internal evidence, dated 1937). He, in turn, suggested that his manuscript and the assignment be turned over to Constance Rourke. Her book, *Charles Sheeler: Artist in the American Tradition,* appeared in August 1938.

In October 1939, New York's Museum of Modern Art presented a major retrospective exhibition of Sheeler's work in painting, drawing, lithography, and photography. The Museum, already a prestigious arbiter of contemporary art, had just opened its 53rd Street building; it had included one-man exhibitions of American artists in its program only a few times. The exhibition was the subject of one of the earliest telecasts on art. At 56, and with 20 years of painting ahead, Sheeler had attained an honored rank among American artists.

Sheeler spent much of 1939 and 1940 "on location" in Colorado, Alabama, and other subject sites for a *Fortune* magazine commission for six paintings on the theme "Power."

1942

Sheeler married for the second time—and changed residence for the last time, moving from Ridgefield to Irvington-on-Hudson, New York. Photography, which had been a minor preoccupation since the early 30s, again provided an auxiliary income. Beginning in 1942, Sheeler worked for the Metropolitan Museum, photographing its collections, largely in support of its enlarged publication program.

95 White Sentinels 1942

Suspended Forms: still life

Sun, Rocks, and Trees: landscape

82 Rocks at Steichen's 1937
conté crayon $10\frac{1}{2} \times 8\frac{3}{4}$
Lent by The Downtown Gallery

91 Steam Turbine 1939

American Interior: interiors

83 Kitchen, Williamsburg 1937
oil on panel 10 x 14
Lent anonymously

86 The Upstairs 1938
oil on canvas 19½ x 12¾
Lent by Cincinnati Art Museum

On the Theme of Farm Buildings: barns

87 Silo 1938
oil on canvas 20 x 19
Lent by Carol Brandt Pavenstedt

93 Shaker Detail 1941
oil and tempera 9 x 10
Lent by The Newark Museum

94 Red against the Light 1942
tempera 8½ x 12¼
Lent by Mr. and Mrs. Anthony Haswell

95 White Sentinels 1942
tempera 14¼ x 21⅛
Lent by Mrs. Edith Gregor Halpert

100 Power House with Trees 1944
tempera 14½ x 21½
Lent by Nathaniel Saltonstall

Skyline: city buildings

92 Neighbors 1940
conté crayon 5 x 4
Lent by The Downtown Gallery

Industrial Architecture: factories and machines

88 Boulder Dam 1939
photograph

89 Installation 1939
photograph

90 Rolling Power 1939
oil on canvas 15 x 30
Lent by Smith College Museum of Art

91 Steam Turbine 1939
oil on canvas 22 x 18
Lent by Butler Institute of American Art

Variations from the Themes

84 Clouds 1937
photograph

85 Portrait circa 1937
photograph

96 Assyrian Relief 1942
photograph

97 Assyrian Relief 1942
photograph

98 The Artist Looks at Nature 1943
oil on canvas 21 x 18
Lent by The Art Institute of Chicago, Gift of the Society for Contemporary American Art
(exhibited in Washington only)

99 Bust of Andrew Jackson 1943
photograph

1945 With the end of the war, Sheeler felt he could return to normalcy, which for him now was painting. He gave up his position with the Metropolitan.

1946-1949 The key events of these years were Sheeler's experiences as artist-in-residence at Phillips Academy, Andover, Massachusetts (October 1946), and the similar residency sponsored by the Currier Gallery in Manchester, New Hampshire (May 1948), which developed from the Andover "experiment." [These events and their implication in the direction Sheeler's painting took thereafter are thoroughly described in Mr. Bartlett Hayes' essay in this catalogue.]

Suspended Forms: still life

108 Classic Still Life 1947
tempera 15½ x 12½
Lent by Mr. and Mrs. Roy R. Neuberger

Sun, Rocks, and Trees: landscape

101 Fissures 1945
watercolor 10¾ x 13¾
Lent by Lane Collection

American Interior: interiors

104 The Yellow Wall 1946
tempera 14 x 11
Lent by Mrs. Edith Gregor Halpert

On the Theme of Farm Buildings: barns

109 Barn Abstraction 1947
tempera 22 x 29½
Lent by Mr. and Mrs. Robert D. Straus

110 On the Theme of Farm Building #2 1947
tempera 8 x 12
Lent by Lane Collection

113 Thunder Shower 1948
tempera 14 x 20
Lent by Mr. and Mrs. James H. Beal

116 Buildings at Lebanon 1949
tempera sight: 13¾ x 19¾
Lent by Walker Art Center

Skyline: city buildings

Industrial Architecture: factories and machines

102 Fugue 1945
oil on canvas 20 x 16
Lent by MacDougall Collection

103 Water 1945
oil on canvas 24 x 29⅛
Lent by The Metropolitan Museum of Art, Arthur H. Hearn Fund

105 Incantation 1946
oil on canvas 24 x 20
Lent by The Brooklyn Museum, Ella C. and John B. Woodward Memorial Funds

106 Ballardvale 1946
oil on canvas 24 x 19
Lent by Addison Gallery of American Art, Phillips Academy, Andover

107 Reflection 1946
ink wash 16¾ x 13⅝
Lent by Charles E. Buckley

111 Architectural Planes 1947
oil on canvas 15 x 12
Lent by Lane Collection

112 Catwalk 1947
oil on canvas 24 x 20
Lent by Charles A. Bauer

114 Amoskeag Canal 1948
oil on canvas 21½ x 23
Lent by The Currier Gallery of Art

115 Amoskeag Mills 1948
oil on canvas 28½ x 24
Lent by Anne Burnett Windfohr

117 Manchester 1949
oil on canvas 25 x 20
Lent by The Baltimore Museum of Art, Edward Joseph Gallagher III Memorial Collection

118 Counterpoint 1949
conté crayon 20 x 28
Lent by Bernard Heineman, Jr.

Variations from the Themes

122 Wings 1949
tempera 16 x 20
Lent by George Hopper Fitch

Suspended Forms: still life

Sun, Rocks, and Trees: landscape

1950-1951 Sheeler's interest in the independent expressive use of photography renewed. Corollary to his studies of Rockefeller Center and the United Nations complex was a revived interest in the cityscape. The building blocks of New York presented a new aspect after the passage of 30 years.

128 Skyline 1950

129 Beech Tree 1951
photograph

130 Beech Tree 1951
photograph

1952 In May Sheeler was in Wisconsin making photographic studies for two corporate commissions. *Convolutions [no. 136]* was executed for the Pabst Brewing Company. He also was in Pittsburgh this year, photographing the blast furnaces. Each new visual experience was eventually carried into paintings.

Sheeler long had had the habit of working out a fully realized miniature painting in watercolor or tempera and then repeating it, with further refinements, in a more conventional scale. Sheeler's spare abstraction of design was the product of intense formal analysis. It is understandable that more than one resolution of an idea might be the outcome: thus the several seemingly identical versions of some works. In the late 40s, when he was exploring a style of superimposed images, Sheeler began using glass panels as a compositional aid. The fragility of the glass was a drawback; William Lane presented him with sheets of plastic as a safer alternative. Now he had a support which offered permanence as well as transparency. Sheeler began using this unusual technical device in the early 50s. Generally, he started a diminutive

American Interior:
interiors

137 Frosted Window circa 1953
photograph

On the Theme of Farm Buildings:
barns

123 Family Group 1950
oil on canvas 15¼ x 29
Lent by Mrs. Ernest Frederick Eidlitz

124 Companions 1950
tempera 12½ x 19½
Lent by Mr. and Mrs. Milton K. Arenberg

133 Conversation Piece 1952
oil on canvas 18 x 25
Lent by Dr. and Mrs. Melvin Boigon

Skyline:
city buildings

125 New York 1950
oil on canvas 13 x 20⅛
Lent by Mr. and Mrs. Karl Swenson

126 RCA Building 1950
photograph

127 Skyline 1950
tempera 1½ x 2½
Lent by Mrs. Edith Gregor Halpert

128 Skyline 1950
oil on canvas 25 x 40
Lent by Wichita Art Museum, Roland P. Murdock Collection
(exhibited in Washington only)

131 New York #2 1951
oil on canvas 27 x 18⅛
Lent by Munson-Williams-Proctor Institute

132 United Nations Building 1951
photograph

134 Convergence 1952
oil on canvas 24 x 16
Lent by Mr. and Mrs. George Greenspan

138 Lever Building 1953
photograph

Industrial Architecture:
factories and machines

119 Variations in Red 1949
oil on canvas 15⅛ x 23¼
Lent by The Toledo Museum of Art

120 Ballardvale Revisited 1949
tempera 15 x 14⅛
Lent by Mr. and Mrs. Anthony Haswell

121 Improvisations on a Mill Town 1949
oil on canvas 29 x 24
Lent by Amon Carter Museum of Western Art

135 Tanks at Cedarburg 1952
photograph

136 Convolutions 1952
oil on canvas 36 x 26
Lent by Illinois Institute of Technology

139 New England Irrelevancies 1953
oil on canvas 29 x 23
Lent by Lane Collection

140 Ore into Iron 1953
oil on canvas 24 x 18
Lent by Lane Collection

Variations from the Themes

Suspended Forms: still life

Sun, Rocks, and Trees: landscape

but complete design in tempera on paper, moved on to a tempera on plexiglass of the same dimensions, next went to the larger oil version, and then returned to the tempera on paper to bring it to completion. This pattern was not invariable, nor did Sheeler feel the need to work out all subjects in multiple versions.

1954 Sheeler was in Los Angeles to attend the opening of the University of California Art Galleries' retrospective exhibition of his work, and from there he went on to San Francisco for a stay of several weeks.

143 Sequoia 1954
photograph

1955-1956 These years are, again, highlighted by travel. A few weeks in the summer of 1955 were spent in John Marin's house in Maine. In the fall Sheeler was in Michigan to study General Motors' new research building designed by Eero Saarinen (Sheeler's favorite architect) for a commissioned painting [no. 151]. From June to August 1956 the Sheelers were on the West Coast, much of the time in San Francisco but visiting Yosemite as well. All of these new visual encounters stimulated fresh creation.

147 Begonias 1955
oil on canvas 25 x 27
Lent by Lane Collection

148 Golden Gate 1955

152 Marin's Rocks 1956
watercolor 10 x 8
Lent by Lane Collection

American Interior: interiors

On the Theme of Farm Buildings: barns

144 Lunenburg 1954
oil on canvas 25 x 34
Lent by Lane Collection

153 On a Shaker Theme 1956
oil on canvas 30 x 36
Lent by Stephen and Sybil Stone Foundation

Skyline: city buildings

Industrial Architecture: factories and machines

141 Aerial Gyrations 1953
oil on canvas 24 x 19
Lent by Dr. and Mrs. Melvin Boigon

142 Steel—Croton 1953
oil on canvas 16 x 24
Lent by Virginia Museum of Fine Arts

145 Architectural Cadences 1954
oil on canvas 25 x 35
Lent by Whitney Museum of American Art

146 Stacks in Celebration 1954
oil on canvas 22 x 28
Lent by Mrs. Otto L. Spaeth

148 Golden Gate 1955
tempera on plexiglass 6¼ x 8½
Lent by National Collection of Fine Arts, Smithsonian Institution

149 The Web 1955
oil on canvas 22 x 24
Lent by Mr. and Mrs. Roy R. Neuberger

150 Western Industrial 1955
oil on canvas 23 x 29
Lent by Mr. and Mrs. Leigh B. Block

151 General Motors Research 1955
oil on canvas 48 x 30
Lent by General Motors Research Laboratories

154 Fisherman's Wharf, San Francisco 1956
tempera on plexiglass 6½ x 4½
Lent by The Downtown Gallery

155 San Francisco 1956
oil on canvas 32 x 22
Lent by The Sara Roby Foundation

Variations from the Themes

My work has continuously been based on a clue seen in Nature from which the subject of a picture may be projected.

Nature, with its profound order, is an inexhaustible source of supply. Its many facets lend themselves freely to all who would help themselves for their particular needs.

Each one may filter out for himself that which is essential to him. Our chief objective is to increase our capacity for perception. The degree of accomplishment determines the calibre of the Artist.

Charles Sheeler
June 1952

In October 1959 Charles Sheeler suffered a stroke which left him unable to paint or use a camera. A second stroke ended his life 7 May 1965.

The above biography is based on evaluation of information in published sources listed in the bibliography to this catalogue. Of unpublished sources, material from Archives of American Art microfilms has been heavily relied upon, especially Sheeler's manuscript autobiography, his letters and scrapbook of press clippings. Information on Sheeler's career in photography was supplied by Mr. Charles Millard.

The quotation from Sheeler concerning his reaction to the 1909 European experience is from the transcript of Mr. Martin Friedman's interview with the artist in 1959, and is used with Mr. Friedman's permission. Sheeler's letter to William Macbeth is contained on Archives microfilm MC11, frames 272–273, and was published by Garnett McCoy in the *Journal of the Archives of American Art* of April 1965. The quotation concerning *Upper Deck* is from a statement in the autobiography, Archives microfilm NSh1, frames 105–107. The quotation from Sheeler of June 1952 is from "The Black Book," printed in its entirety in this catalogue.

ABIGAIL BOOTH

Suspended Forms: still life

Sun, Rocks, and Trees: landscape

156 The Great Tree 1957
tempera 4¾ x 6½
Lent by Dr. and Mrs. Herbert J. Kayden

157 The Great Tree 1957
tempera 4¾ x 6½
Lent by The Downtown Gallery

158 Yosemite #2 1957
tempera 6½ x 9½
Lent by William H. Lane Foundation

169 Sun, Rocks and Trees 1959
tempera 6¾ x 9¾
Lent by Mr. and Mrs. George Perutz

American Interior: interiors

On the Theme of Farm Buildings: barns

159 Two against the White 1957
tempera $14\frac{7}{8}$ x 18
Lent by The Downtown Gallery

160 Two against the White 1957
tempera 15 x 18
Lent by Hallmark Cards, Inc.

161 Red against the White 1957
tempera on plexiglass $4\frac{7}{8}$ x 6
Lent by Museum of Fine Arts, Boston, Abraham Shuman Fund

166 On a Connecticut Theme 1958
oil on canvas 19 x 29
Lent by Lawrence H. Bloedel

167 Composition around Red (Pennsylvania) 1958
oil on canvas 26 x 33
Lent by The Downtown Gallery

168 Hex Signs 1958
tempera $7\frac{1}{2}$ x 10
Lent by Stephen and Sybil Stone Foundation

170 Composition around White 1959
oil on canvas 30 x 33
Lent by Mr. and Mrs. Malcolm G. Chace, Jr.

Skyline: city buildings

Industrial Architecture: factories and machines

162 California Industrial 1957
oil on canvas $25\frac{1}{2}$ x $33\frac{1}{2}$
Lent by Mr. and Mrs. John S. Hilson

163 Continuity 1957
tempera on plexiglass 10 x 8
Lent by Dr. Walter Myden

164 Continuity #2 1957
tempera $9\frac{1}{2}$ x $7\frac{1}{2}$
Lent by Mrs. Agnes E. Meyer

165 Continuity 1957
oil on canvas 29 x 23
Lent by Fort Worth Art Association, Gift of William E. Scott Foundation

168 Hex Signs 1958

Variations from the Themes

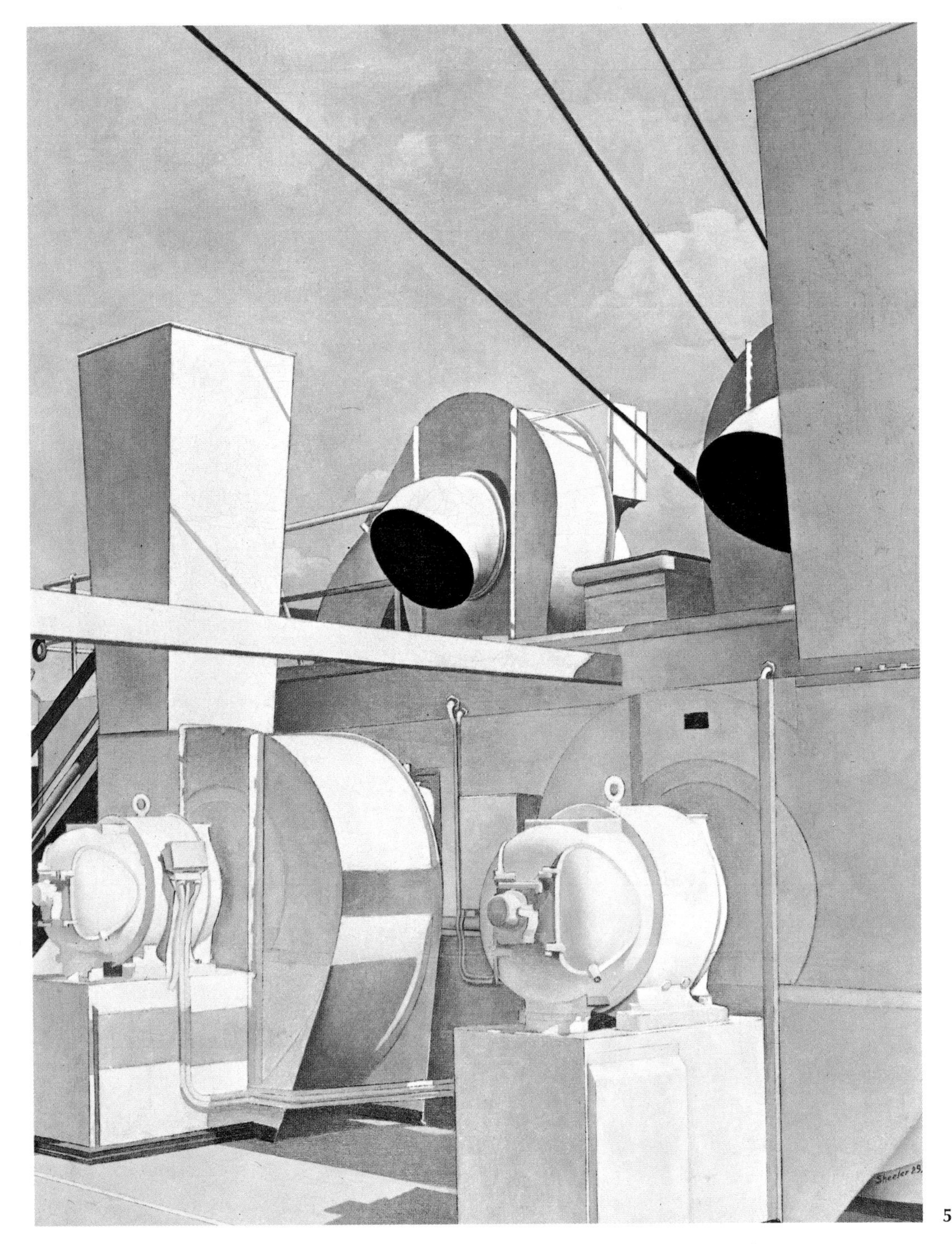

54 Upper Deck 1929

Sheeler had an uncomplicated, factual world view and regarded his painting pragmatically, free of romantic or obscure overtones. In this efficient view, there was little room for experimentation; there could be no evidence of any hesitation in achieving the final result. A compulsion about clarity and order permeates Sheeler's work, and throughout his long production he never relaxed self-imposed standards of organization and "finish."

Sheeler's personal detachment pervades his art. Essentially he was the anonymous, but acutely selective, observer who always remained outside of the subjects he analyzed and reordered. Such self-insulation and self-protection seem to have been a life pattern. An amiable personality, he was nevertheless an isolated personality, reticent in his associations with other artists. During his New York residence from 1919 to 1927, although respected by important collectors and dealers, he remained a peripheral figure in the art world.

The partisan of new European painting, Arthur B. Davies, befriended Sheeler and invited him to submit six works, including the Cezanne-influenced *White Tulips*, to the 1913 Armory show, the American section of which Davies helped organize. Sheeler, however, remained outside Davies' cosmopolitan scene. At the free-wheeling salons of the eminent collector and patron of modernism, Walter Arensberg, Sheeler was an interested, if passive, observer in conversations that raged about new literature, Dada, and other heady and current artistic phenomena. Among the many Americans contributing to these animated discussions were Isadora Duncan, William Carlos Williams, Amy Lowell, Joseph Stella, and Charles Demuth, and Arensberg's European "regulars," including Duchamp, Gleizes, Picabia, and Crôti. Sheeler regarded most of the Europeans and their projects—especially the Dada ventures—with tolerant amusement, tinged with suspicion. He had a prim attitude about glib foreigners whose conversation, usually in French which he did not understand, rarely included him; his relationship with them was, at best, tenuous ("They didn't know I existed!"). Only Duchamp seems to have taken some polite interest in the young American's work, and if Sheeler never comprehended the mysteries of Dada, he was at least mildly intrigued by the Frenchman's cryptic "readymades"—a light bulb filled with the air of Paris, a small cage containing marble "sugar" cubes. Sheeler, an archetype of the provincial American painter, remained on the sidelines of the internationalist discussions at the Arensbergs'. But his own art, after 1920, became central to an important new American direction—the Precisionist view.

In 1959, while preparing the exhibition "The Precisionist View in American Art," the writer had conversations and correspondence with Charles Sheeler. Quotations from Sheeler in this essay are from transcripts of those interviews and letters, except where cited as from Constance Rourke's biography, *Charles Sheeler: Artist in the American Tradition*.

THE ART OF CHARLES SHEELER: AMERICANA IN A VACUUM

10 Landscape 1915

14 Flower Forms 1917

SHEELER AND THE PRECISIONISTS

During the 20s the Precisionist attitude made its unheralded appearance in the work of a number of American painters, most of whom resided in New York. The adjective "Precisionist" was used by writers—especially Henry McBride—to characterize a rigorous, sharply defined painting style that ranged from photographic realism to abstraction applied to themes derived from the American environment. "Immaculate" and "Cubist-Realist" are other general terms used to describe the styles of the group. Initially associated with this direction in the 20s were George Ault, Henry Billings, Francis Criss, Stuart Davis, Charles Demuth, Preston Dickinson, Elsie Driggs, Charles Goeller, Stephen Hirsch, Louis Lozowick, Georgia O'Keeffe, Morton Schamberg, Charles Sheeler, Niles Spencer, and Joseph Stella.

The paintings of Charles Sheeler and Georgia O'Keeffe, over a period of more than 40 years, virtually defined the Precisionists' full thematic and stylistic range. Joseph Stella's Futurist visions of bridges and Stuart Davis' early syncopated abstractions of cement mixers and city streets are closely related to this identifiable, if never formally declared, direction. Charles Demuth's faceted images of Pennsylvania grain elevators, Peter Blume's dehumanized factories, and Niles Spencer's ochreous city abstractions are central to it. While most artists initially associated with the Precisionist development in the 20s later varied their styles—moving in and out of abstraction—a hard clarity and formulism persisted in their work. Although neither Sheeler nor O'Keeffe ever accepted complete abstraction, in their later painting both simplified their forms radically.

No group philosophy, program, or manifestoes characterized the Precisionist phenomenon. Nor were all of the artists associated with it ever acquainted, but several found themselves exhibiting in group shows with the same few pioneering dealers, primarily Alfred Stieglitz, Stephen Bourgeois, and Charles Daniel. Ultimately, the Downtown Gallery, established in 1926 by Edith Halpert, became a significant force for this style, sponsoring the painting of Sheeler, O'Keeffe, and many other Precisionist artists. Sheeler joined the Gallery in 1931. Other galleries sponsoring Precisionist artists included J. B. Neumann, the Montross Gallery, Rehn Gallery, and the Whitney Studio Club.

Paradoxically, the Precisionist style, so intimately related to the evolution of modernism in America, was basically a conservative, scourging phenomenon. It offered an alternative to anecdotal American regionalist painting and, through its abstracting and classicizing aspects, removed itself entirely from any topicality. But, as Sheeler's art demonstrates, the regionalist strain remained crucial to it. The involvement with the cityscape and the farm theme persisted, and no amount of adaptation of European stylistic approaches was able to divest this rigorous American idiom of its fundamental colloquialism.

In Precisionist paintings the world is static. Sheeler's unpopulated landscapes and cityviews are eternalized visions, safe from the erosion of time and nature. Even

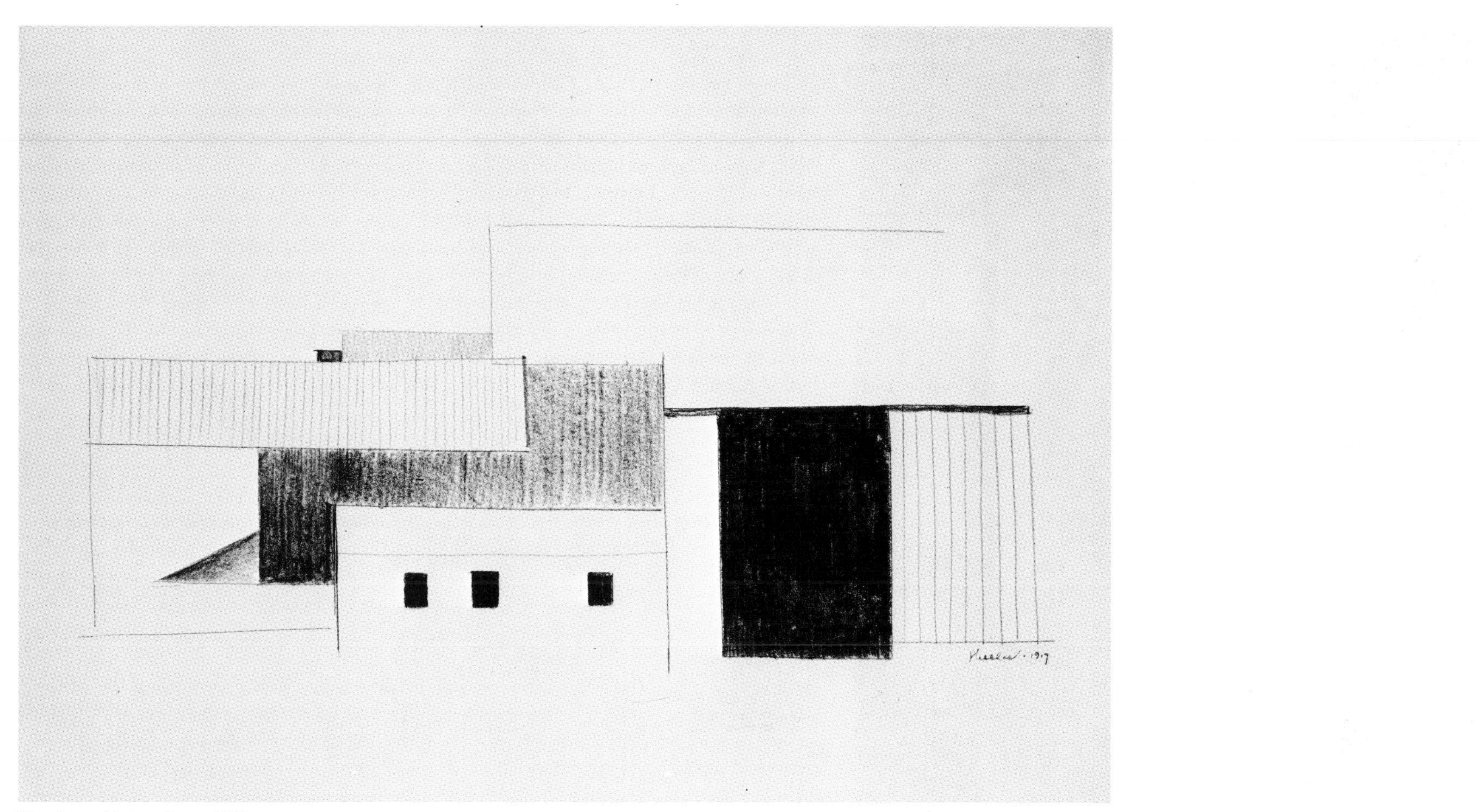

15 Barn Abstraction 1917

O'Keeffe's sun-bleached animal skulls exist outside of time, and she rendered decay and death pristinely. If, on rare occasions, a human figure did intrude into a Precisionist painting, it was chiefly as a formal element that heightened the sense of total dehumanization.

For Sheeler and other Precisionist painters, the constant peril was an absolute sterile imagery. Sheeler accepted this risk and virtually built his art on an impersonal view—coolness remained the basis of his painting. Although younger American artists such as Ralston Crawford and Niles Spencer were attracted by his obsessive clarity, Sheeler was no teacher, proselytizer, or theorist. Although he shared exhibitions with the other Precisionists, he had no sustained friendships with any of them. For example, between Sheeler and O'Keeffe, who represent the core of the Precisionist direction, there was respect but little communication—besides, they never

20 Hallway 1919

regarded themselves as following similar directions.

Precisionist painting, by definition, is anti-expressionistic. During the last few years of Sheeler's life, Abstract Expressionism was the prevailing American mode; he considered it undisciplined and overstated, but, nevertheless, responded to some of its imagery. About his own work he was so compulsive that he frequently spoke of the need for a complete plan before beginning every picture to assure a totally pure final result. More complicated paintings sometimes were preceded by small, carefully detailed color studies, and during his later years he worked with tempera on small plexiglass panels, making compositional and color changes by simply wiping the panel clean. He had a fine workman's sensibility about his product, and the "artist-craftsman" dualism in his personality never seems to have concerned him. He tried to eliminate all traces of the painting process, including brushstrokes: "I just don't want to see any more than is absolutely necessary of the physical materials that go into a picture."

INFLUENCES—EUROPEAN ART AND PHOTOGRAPHY

Whatever innovative formalist philosophy characterized Precisionist painting was assimilated from European examples. Synthesizers of existing ideas, the Precisionists incorporated certain French approaches and mannerisms in their representations of the American environment. Cubism was their major source. Some had seen it developing in Europe—Demuth and Dickinson visited Paris before 1910. For Sheeler and the Precisionists it became, eventually, a strong pragmatic discipline, but without the theoretical character of its original manifestation; and, by the time the Americans absorbed it, Cubism, a short-lived style, had hardened into a diagrammatic idiom.

Sheeler had been in Europe briefly in 1909, and had seen Cubist paintings at the collector Michael Stein's house. For all his essentially provincial attitudes, he was quickly convinced that Picasso was modernism's dominant figure, and after his return to the United States, began painting landscapes and still lifes utilizing Cezannesque and Cubist idioms. The effect of the 1913 Armory show was to heighten his interest in Cubism, and he explored various aspects of this quickly internationalized style. *Landscape,* 1915 [no. 10, illustrated], was conceived within a strongly defined Cubist structure, and *Flower Forms,* 1917 [no. 14, illustrated], is a rhythmic, extremely simplified abstraction, the organic contours and almost anatomical treatment of the flower theme strongly suggesting O'Keeffe's later botanical paintings. *Barn Abstraction* [no. 15, illustrated], a conté drawing of the same year, consists entirely of overlaid rectangles. Cubist techniques never left his work—strong, simple planes and volumes, exceptional formalism, even flattened perspective and shallow space characterize his most literal interiors, such as *Americana* and *View of New York* [no. 62, illustrated], both done in 1931.

Sheeler's subjects were, in themselves, often cubistic forms. He selected them for their inherent abstract quality and then further abstracted them by eliminating all disturbing complexity and carefully relating these forms to their austere surroundings. Analytical processes always prevailed in his work, even in the early 20s when he abandoned standard Cubist procedures such as arbitrary lines across the picture plane and virtually monochromatic, volume-building, brush strokes. In the mid 40s, however, Sheeler returned to some of these approaches, using them in a semi-diagrammatic and posteresque manner in such works as *Manchester,* 1949 [no. 117, illustrated, page 77], a view of buildings bordering a canal in that New Hampshire textile town.

It is generally understood that Cubism was germinal to Sheeler's style but, in an almost subliminal way, so was Surrealism. Only those American artists who had close contact with Surrealism's European progenitors really comprehended its neurotic mystique. The virtuosity and polished technique of this arcane mode attracted a number of American painters, but their "magic realism" was a far cry from the Surrealist message. Pragmatic and nonmystical as he was, Sheeler's windowless buildings, streets extending toward infinity, and hermetic landscapes are related to the imagery of Surrealist "hand-painted" dreams. Sheeler was always fascinated by the enigmatic aspects of the staircase, a favorite Surrealist subject and a persistent theme in his photographs and paintings, and *Hallway,* 1919 [no. 20, illustrated], with its stairwell reminiscent of classical architecture suggests a De Chirico interior. (Other important staircase paintings by Sheeler include *Stairway to Studio,* 1924; *Staircase, Doylestown,* 1925; and *The Upstairs,* 1938 [nos. 36, 43, and 86, illustrated].) A strong sense of the metaphysical characterizes *Self Portrait* [no. 32, illustrated, page 69], a 1923 conté drawing of a telephone before a window, in which part of Sheeler's body is dimly reflected, barely perceptible, suggesting an ectoplasmic form. Duchamp liked this drawing, perhaps for its cryptic, nonartistic subject—the telephone being a ubiquitous, utilitarian object close to his own "ready-mades."

One of Sheeler's most enigmatic paintings, *The Artist Looks at Nature,* 1943 [no. 98, illustrated, page 67], is strongly reminiscent of classical Surrealism. In it, Sheeler is seen, his back to the viewer, seated at an easel on a parapet overlooking a bucolic landscape divided into walled areas like a vista in a medieval book of hours. Paradoxically, this landscape bears no relationship to the farmhouse interior he shows himself depicting. In this strange, provocative painting, Sheeler is working on his well-known drawing *Interior with Stove,* 1932 [no. 67, illustrated, page 70]. Sheeler considered *The Artist Looks at Nature* a sport, an unusual digression in his depersonalized imagery, and minimized its metaphysical connotations.

Mysticism held little interest for Sheeler, and he also considered any similarities between his work and classical Surrealism to be purely fortuitous. Not that he was hostile to this style—for example, he admired Pierre Roy's work, but probably for the same reason, he liked William Harnett's *trompe l'oeil* still lifes. He maintained he was not interested in subconscious expression and that nothing existed in his paintings not immediately perceivable. His vocabulary of forms was based on objects and surroundings he knew well, whether historical or industrial shapes. Strong, basic form and the implication of efficiency were requirements for their selection, and

36 Stairway to Studio 1924

86 The Upstairs 1938

43 Staircase, Doylestown 1925

24 Church Street E1 1920

Sheeler affirmed that his subjects had no connotation beyond their immediate function.

Inevitably, he chose inherently functional subjects: a barn, an oil refinery, a colonial kitchen, or the equipment in a photographer's studio, but even these everyday objects and surroundings—so compulsively presented—can, in the blinding clarity of Sheeler's presentation, sometimes evoke a sense of the metaphysical. While Sheeler's art lacks the choked silence of Magritte's paintings, its anonymity of subject and occasional visionary quality can be as haunting as Magritte's world. His staircases, half-open doors, and vacuum-like landscapes were presented in low key, but with extraordinary presence. If Sheeler is enigmatic in such works, he is never menacing. Unlike O'Keeffe's iconography of desolation with its whitened, animal skulls and crosses of the *penitentes*, Sheeler's imagery is essentially innocent, almost naive. Yet it seems more than a coincidence that the hallucinating visions of the Surrealists were evolving at the same time as photographic hyper-realism in his own work.

Sheeler's photographic experience was, of course, central to development of his painting style. He worked as a photographer, with Edward Steichen, on *Vogue* magazine and supported himself photographing art objects for galleries. His exhibition at the De Zayas Gallery in 1920 included photographs of industrial sites and African sculptures as well as paintings. Once he had established himself as a painter, he preferred to de-emphasize the relationship of photography to his painting, but parallels and relationships are obvious.

The violent perspective of buildings seen from high above in *Church Street El*, 1920 [no. 24, illustrated], is closely related to Sheeler's one cinematic venture, a film he made with Paul Strand called *Manhatta*, dealing with New York skyscrapers. The film's sharp focus and its closeup and exaggerated perspective angles were to be reiterated in future paintings. Even Sheeler's color was affected by his photographic eye. Generally tonal and muted, it was a carryover from his black and white photography. Color always remained a secondary quality in his paintings; he used it quietly, and in no way does it contradict form or value structure. In fact, Sheeler is frequently at his best in totally black and white drawings—his masterful conté studies, *Interior, Bucks County Barn,* 1932, and *Of Domestic Utility,* 1933 [nos. 68, 70, illustrated], are equal to any of his paintings of the period.

Photography continued to play a crucial role in his development as a painter. The 1927 assignment to photographically document Ford's River Rouge plant led to such later works as *American Landscape,* 1930 [no. 59, illustrated], *Classic Landscape,* 1931 [no. 63, illustrated], and *City Interior,* 1936 *[illustrated].* Especially in the mid 30s his photographic technique affected his painting style.

Sheeler had definite ideas about segregating his painting and photography: "Photography is nature seen from the eyes outward, painting from the eyes inward. No matter how objective a painter's work may seem to be, he draws upon a store of images upon which his mind has worked. Photography records inalterably the single image, while painting records a plurality of images willfully directed by the artist." (Rourke, p. 119.)

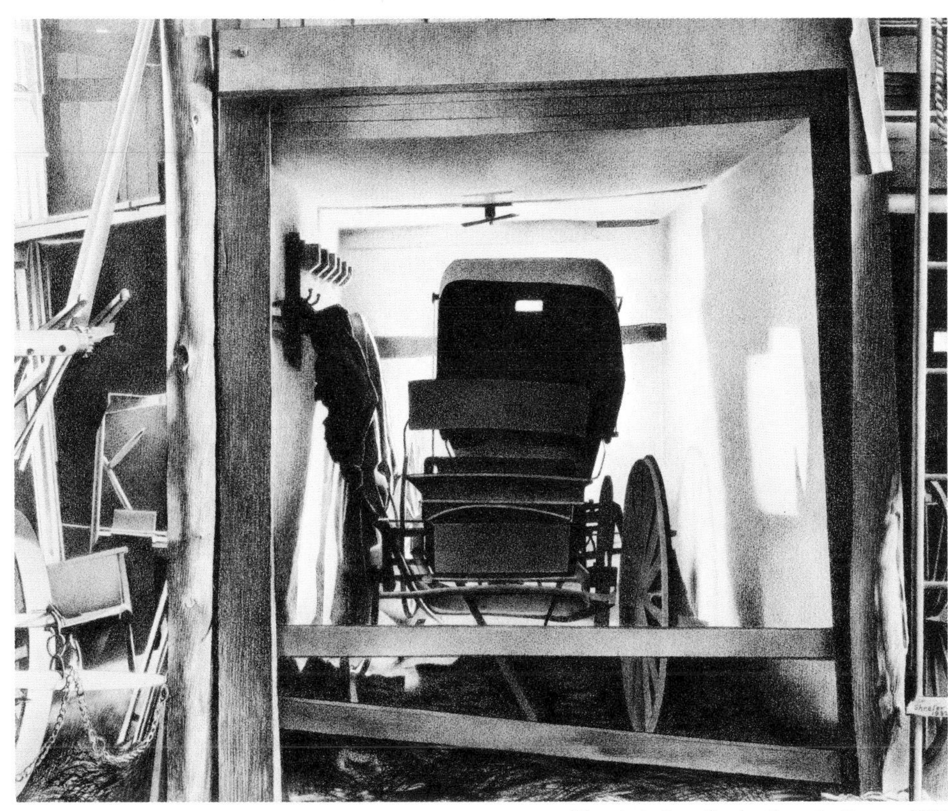

68 Interior, Bucks County Barn 1932

70 Of Domestic Utility 1933

SHEELER'S STYLISTIC EVOLUTION

Sheeler virtually defined his range of themes and set the abstract and realistic limits of his style during the 20s; the next thirty years were an elaboration of these ideas. Although his approach evolved from a modified abstraction in the early 20s, to realism beginning in the 30s, and back to abstraction in the late 40s, it did so with great consistency and with no abrupt shifts.

After his various Cubist experiments, his identifiable style developed in taut, sharp-edged paintings of Bucks County barns, still lifes, and New York buildings. *Pertaining to Yachts and Yachting,* 1922 [no. 28, illustrated], is a key early work, not only for its unusual subject in Sheeler's *oeuvre* (he was no sportsman) but also for its overall, rhythmic organization. Composed of intersecting curvilinear forms derived from sail patterns, it is a frozen attempt to convey movement of boats in a Futurist manner. Sheeler, however, was never comfortable with the idea of dynamism, and quickly returned to his static world. The small *Still Life,* 1925 [no. 40, illustrated], is a concise harmonization of fastidious rendering and abstraction. In this skillfully centralized

59 American Landscape 1930

63 Classic Landscape 1931

composition, a plate of apples is neatly positioned on a rectangle of blue paper; a deep-belled, transparent goblet and a wine glass are in diagonal opposition. Perspective is arbitrary, and deep space is sacrificed in favor of tipped-up, flattened planes in this modest but stylistically forceful picture. Controlled arrangements like these were Sheeler's strength, each object being chosen for its elementary contours and adaptability to placement in careful, formal juxtaposition with others and within the total environment.

By the late 20s, Sheeler's work moved toward even more heightened realism; and, in this respect, he was the most accomplished of the Precisionists, using his uncanny ability to render form in virtually the manner of 17th-century Dutch painting. In 1929, Sheeler painted *Upper Deck* [no. 54, illustrated], a coolly toned picture and a pivotal work. Its abstract realism and solid geometry of mechanical forms make it a prototype of all paintings of technological themes. *Upper Deck* is one of the most distinguished examples of Sheeler's commanding ability to select, arrange, and realistically present a subject. With this painting, Sheeler said he had arrived at the working method he could use throughout his life. It was the making of highly detailed preliminary studies—"an engineer's plan," as he described it. The final structure and appearance of the painting was fully determined before the canvas was begun. *Upper Deck* illustrates Sheeler's ability to analyze the geometric structure of mechanical forms; this quest always remained central to his work.

Sometimes, Sheeler was not entirely successful in asserting the underlying abstract structure of his subjects and many industrial paintings became exercises in virtuosity, lacking the formal power of *City Interior* or *Upper Deck*. In certain works of the 30s, Sheeler sacrificed abstract structure to complex literalism. The River Rouge factory paintings, for example, are technically brilliant but, at most, are idealized industrial vistas, more concerned with description than with strong plastic qualities. Unfortunately, he was too often overwhelmed by such complex subjects and his best resolutions were of simpler configurations, whether buildings or objects in a room.

Incantation, 1946 [no. 105, illustrated], based on enormous spheres and cylinders of an oil refinery, is Sheeler's most imposing industrial image. By its elementary volumes and strong tubular forms—alluding to Léger's handling of similar themes—*Incantation* illustrates Sheeler's art at a perfect equilibrium of literal and abstract elements. In several subsequent industrial paintings, especially some undertaken as commissions, he failed to achieve this crucial synthesis.

All objects in Sheeler's paintings are treated with equal gravity and sharp clarity, none is diminished in importance through placement or indistinct handling. His interiors are never in disarray. He did not happen upon a theme or situation; rather, a few distinct objects are arranged in careful equilibrium to form his composition—no accidents, no contradictory forms are allowed to intrude, and everything represented is carefully subordinated to the overall geometric logic of the composition. He remained concerned with exquisite placement, and probably no American artist since Whistler had been so involved with such delicately calibrated positioning of objects in sparse interiors. This quality of organizing a few dominant forms in strong

City Interior 1936 Collection: Worcester Art Museum (not exhibited)

28 Pertaining to Yachts and Yachting 1922

abstract relationships characterizes *View of New York,* 1931 [no. 62, illustrated]. Four major shapes—a window, a photographer's table, chair, and lamp—are presented with sharp simplicity as elements floated on a vertical-horizontal grid. (Sheeler often resolved the disposition of a vast number of objects by using them as elements on an invisible grid, as in *Kitchen, Williamsburg,* 1937 [no. 83, illustrated]. Although some sensation of deep space persists, the furniture, pots, and pans are grouped on a vertical-horizontal axis.) The lamp, chair, and table are flattened, and presented as though on the same transparent plane in front of the window. A slight variation on this composition characterizes the placement of the two photography lamps and plant in *Cactus,* also 1931 [no. 60, illustrated]. Aside from their similar rigorous, compositional qualities, the two pictures are related in that they introduce an autobiographical note; they depict his photographic equipment in his Beaux Arts studio in New York. Sheeler's professional involvement as a photographer was strong at this time, and his direct use of these cold studio forms was, to say the least, innovative.

Sheeler's highly accomplished brand of selective realism reaches ultimate refinement in *Rolling Power,* 1939 [no. 90, illustrated], a remarkable rendering of locomotive wheels seen absolutely parallel to the picture plans; its ultra reality is harmonized with the strong abstract structure of the wheels and other mechanical forms.

The dynamism and tense spatial sensation of Sheeler's early pictures rarely occurred in his later abstractions. *Manchester,* a crucial painting, illustrates the paradoxes in Sheeler's approach: volume versus two-dimensional form, description versus generalization. *Manchester* is a successful resolution, but in the late 40s Sheeler's failures were chiefly those paintings in which the pragmatic and the analytical aspects of his temperament warred. In several works of the early 50s, this dichotomy became acute; it is evident in several barn paintings of the period, in which Cubist-style diagonal lines careen across volumetric details of silos and brick walls. In such a picture, a sense of control always remains, but one feels that Sheeler is frequently caught within his own formulae. Space in many of these later pictures is not so much ambiguous as indecisive, despite Sheeler's consistent clarity of execution. He escapes from over-conventionalization in *Architectural Cadences,* 1954 [no. 145, illustrated], which, for all its flattened, posteresque character, is an effective picture that misses the trap of its own stylistic cliché.

Sheeler, in his later years, continued to produce significant, lucid pictures, but his production as a whole, definitely showed his realist and formalist proclivities. In a number of paintings of the 50s, including *Architectural Cadences* and *Aerial Gyrations,* 1953 [no. 141, illustrated], Sheeler employed a procedure derived from photographic double exposures. For example, the skyline in *Architectural Cadences* virtually repeats itself in a bluish variation, and the blast furnaces in *Aerial Gyrations* are echoed as pale, spectral images. Sheeler said that some of his multiple image paintings combined forms from a repertory of sites he had previously painted, certain shapes having imprinted themselves deeply in his memory. Most important, Sheeler's late style of diagrammatic realism could be very authoritative, as evidenced in *On a Shaker Theme,* 1956 [no. 153, illustrated]. Based on a Hancock, Massachusetts, structure, it is

40 Still Life 1925

105 Incantation 1946

62 View of New York 1931

60 Cactus 1931

83 Kitchen, Williamsburg 1937

composed entirely of modified rectangular planes, and in its purity suggests the best of early European Constructivist works.

THE RURAL AND URBAN AMERICAN ENVIRONMENT

Implicitly an artist of the "American scene," Sheeler defines this genre's clinical extreme in his painting. Social realism dominated American painting in the 30s, and the Precisionists' timeless, glacial vision seems diametrically opposed to this trend. Yet, the social realists and Precisionists alike were engaged in an insular expression which exalted the native environment. No amount of simplification or arbitrary disposition of forms obscured the typical Sheeler theme, by then almost wholly architectural subjects such as barns and massive industrial complexes. Sheeler always portrayed specific places, even in his quasi-abstract style of the 40s in which elements of different locales were overlaid.

Sheeler's interest in American historical themes began in 1910 when he rented a small, mid-18th century farmhouse near Doylestown, Pennsylvania. Solidly built and sparsely furnished, it served as a studio for himself and for his friend Morton Scham-

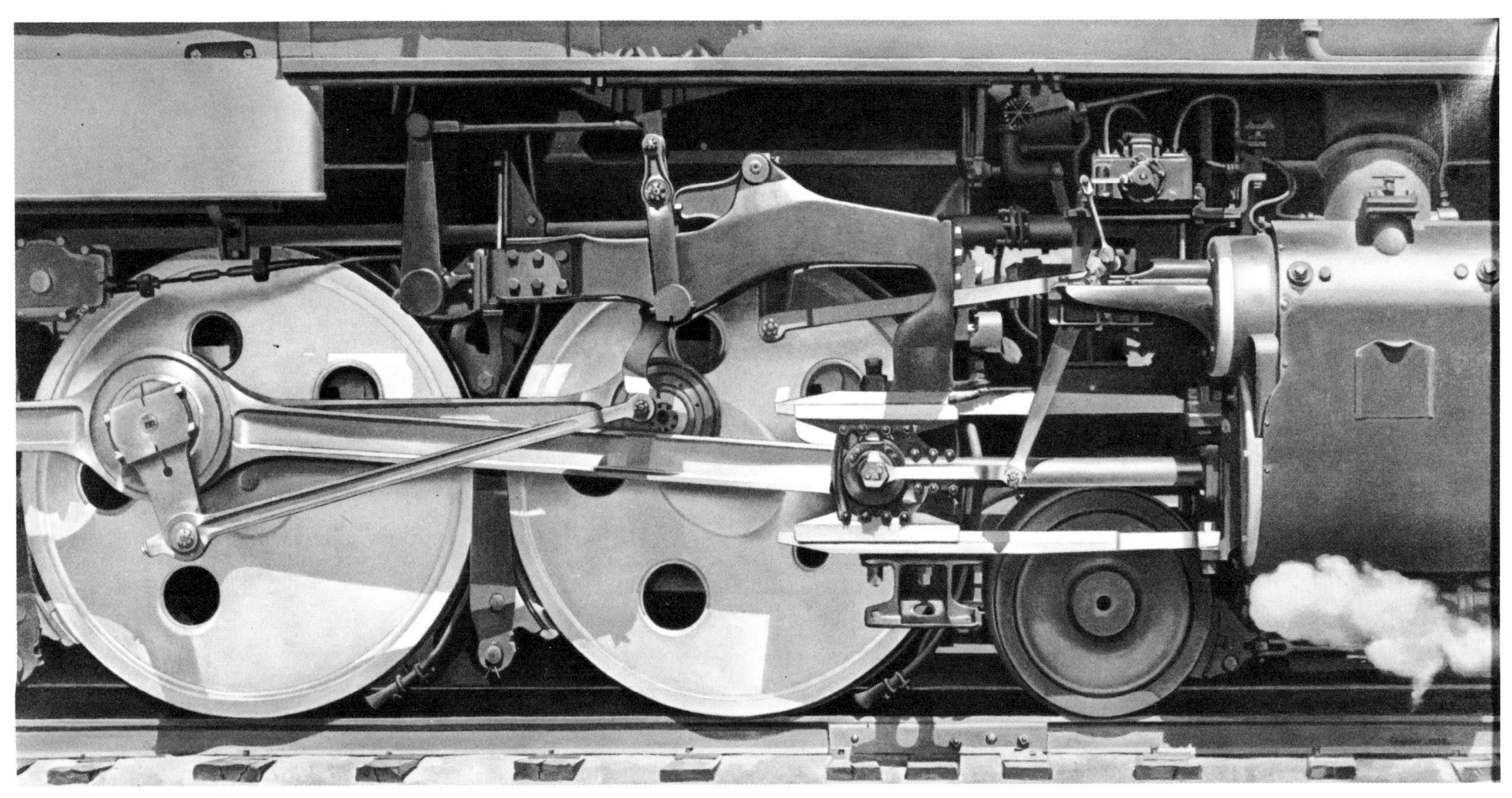

90 Rolling Power 1939

145 Architectural Cadences 1954

berg. They sketched and painted around the countryside, often visiting the nearby Bucks County museum to study its collection of rural Americana. In various houses in which Sheeler lived were Shaker chairs, cabinets, and tables. The simple shapes of this furniture appear in *Americana* and *Home Sweet Home,* 1931 [no. 61, illustrated]. The main room of Sheeler's last residence in Irvington-on-Hudson, a gray stone house called "Birdsnest," contained Shaker pieces and early American glass; the rugs and couch pillows were of rectangular checker and plaid patterns like those in his interior paintings, and its severely geometric stairway immediately recalls the Doylestown interiors. With little modification, Sheeler's environments traveled with him for some 40 years.

The Doylestown experience formed much of Sheeler's early style, providing him with many recurrent themes. At ease in a passive, rural environment, he would have remained for longer periods at this weekend house except for the necessity of earning a living in Philadelphia as an architectural photographer. He made frequent trips to New York to see exhibitions and work on photographic assignments, but never was really at home in the city. In 1927 he sought the seclusion of the country and suc-

141 Aerial Gyrations 1953

153 On a Shaker Theme 1956

61 Home Sweet Home 1931

cessively located in relatively remote areas just outside of New York City: South Salem, New York; Ridgefield, Connecticut; and, finally, Irvington-on-Hudson, New York.

The Precisionists were as regional in their outlook as Benton, Curry, Wood, and Marsh, who romanticized Iowa farms, Kansas prairies, and New York tenements. Sheeler was the most classical of the regionalists. He shared their American subject, eternalizing it by eliminating the transient distractions of human presence, and his sparse images idealize both the bountiful countryside and the geometrically ordered city.

Invariably, Sheeler is regarded as an "artist in the American tradition" (this phrase was the subtitle of Constance Rourke's 1938 biography), devoting himself to fastidious representations of indigenous themes. The implication is that he extends the clear-eyed, pragmatic traditions of American primitive painters, and of Feke, Copley, Bingham, Homer, and Eakins.

In many respects Sheeler fits the characterization as a genuine national product, but there are some sharp contradictions. Despite his attachment to American subject matter, he was not an unqualified admirer of those artists whose tradition he presumably extends. For Sheeler, Homer's realism was that of "the stage drop," Eakins "had a sense of craft but it was mainly clinical," and Bingham "leaves nature where he finds it without that plus which represents what the great artist sees." (Rourke, pp. 184, 185). His "put-down" of these major American figures may seem surprising but he genuinely believed that their art lacked a steady purifying force. Historical American subject matter—midwestern barns and colonial Williamsburg—were his archaistic themes, but Sheeler never regarded himself as either a folk artist or historian. His preferences were decidedly for Cezanne and Picasso, strange choices for a "professional Yankee" painter but logical ones for an artist strongly concerned with formal structure.

Sheeler was as interested in modern America as in the agrarian past, and a remarkable series of industrial paintings supports this. Technology became a crucial ingredient in early-20th-century European and American art, and the Precisionists were among the first to incorporate the machine as a major theme. Generally the American artist's approach to technology was far more literal than the European's. In Europe, Gabo, Pevsner, and the German Bauhaus artists, envisaging some mystical fusion of aesthetics and technology, experimented with industrial materials to evolve a purely abstract machine art. Not all Europeans took technology so seriously. Léger derived syncopated, polychromed shapes from the industrial landscape and wittily "tubularized" the human figure; Picabia transmuted machines into personages and Duchamp invented esoteric physical laws for his images.

For Sheeler the industrial theme was central to his concept of Americana, equal in importance to his idealized pastorales. He had explored the forms of factories, locomotives, cranes, and oil refineries in photographs before they became painting subjects.

Sheeler's hermetic visualizations of the city's geometry had no connection with its daily life. Its factories, bridges, gigantic cranes, ore boats, and locomotives existed without human presence. All components of the industrial environment were processed through his vision with equal clarity and dispassion, the same attention given to a wraith of chimney smoke as to a gigantic grain elevator.

His true subject matter, beyond the forms described, was efficiency and harmony. Social considerations were not part of his painting philosophy. "Sheeler approaches the industrial landscape, whether it be farm buildings, textile mills or oil refineries with the same sort of piety Fra Angelico used toward angels. His architecture remains pure and uncontaminated by any trace of humans or human activities, an industrialist's heaven where factories work themselves. In revealing the beauty of factory architecture, Sheeler has become the Raphael of the Fords. Who is it that will be the Giotto of the U.A.W.?" asked Charles Corwin *(New York Daily Worker,* 4 February 1949). And, of Sheeler's industrial complex, *City Interior,* 1936, Winslow Ames said, "It is not industry as industry seems, but (to paraphrase Kipling) the industry of our dreams, in which are mingled Manifest Destiny, the grandeur and loneliness of the prairies, and the old-fashioned immigrants' belief in sidewalks paved with gold" (*Worcester Art Museum Annual,* 1936-1937, p. 97).

Although the geometry of industrial forms fascinated him, he was also impressed with the power structure that generated and sustained the industrial complexes he idealized. His admiration for industry and its power figures were touchingly naive—but complete. Sheeler greatly respected the industrialist, and his photographic and painting commissions brought him into frequent contact with industry's movers and shakers. Instead of portraits of industrial barons, Sheeler painted their domains.

A strongly moralistic attitude characterizes Sheeler's choice of subjects. In his paintings, American functionalism and basic verities merge with technological efficiency (for him, the best of all possible worlds.) His art implies a direct connection between pre-industrial America and present-day technological efficiency.

Sheeler painted a universe whose various elements relate in perfect harmony. No storm clouds appear in his blue skies; the time of day is never certain. It is always a perfect day. No sign of deterioration is permitted, even in depiction of historical subjects; his portrayals of old barns avoid the picturesque sentimentalism inherent in such subjects; every field is green in his Arcadia. The time is now—the idealized present.

There is a strong contemporary sensibility in Sheeler's painting. It shares many of the qualities of present-day formalism, and emphasizes an aesthetic of austerity which most younger artists understand. Like many of them, Sheeler was a rigorous formalist who eliminated nonessentials. Irreducible man-made forms, anonymous surfaces, and, above all, cool imagery make him interesting to a new generation of geometrically oriented artists, even though his literalism is foreign to them. Sheeler—the inveterate classicist—synthesizes and corrects nature, eliminates imperfection, and subtly readjusts the world.

MARTIN FRIEDMAN

106 Ballardvale 1946

REMINISCENCE

A man's life is cumulative, like the human brain itself, and to understand wholly the work and character of anyone is to examine his entirety. Because this is impossible for me to accomplish, I intend to dwell only on fragmentary aspects of my own association with Charles Sheeler, hoping to provide an inkling of a species of friendship which covered almost a quarter of a century.

It began at the Art Institute of Chicago in the fall of 1943. As members of a jury invited to select the entries and allocate awards at the annual exhibit of painting by living American artists, we rapidly learned to alter our initial mode of formal address. Charles was a man easy to befriend, if there was a common ground for communication. We communicated not only during the intensive discriminations of the jury work itself, but also in those happily relaxed intervals provided by the hospitality of the Institute. As Charles himself might have put it, "You never know what may come along to influence you, no more than you may know what sort of an influence you are; you can merely hope for the best and yourself do the best you can, otherwise it isn't worth very much." He was colloquial in his philosophy, which is, perhaps, what made him the ready and thoughtful philosopher and friend which he was to so many.

Kindly and speculative, he was yet a person of positive convictions, especially as these were related to aesthetic matters. One of the incidents which attracted me most to him at that first meeting (apart from the gay charm of his wife, Musya, who participated in those intervals just mentioned) came from his conviction about the merits of a painting by Marsden Hartley (one of the last painted before that artist's death a few days before). The jury had awarded it first prize without equivocation. Subsequently, however, the jury was instructed by the Institute staff that although the painting had been selected by Hartley himself for submission to the exhibit, and was therefore eligible for inclusion, it was *hors de concours* for a monetary award which, by terms of exhibition rules, was intended to serve the needs of a living artist. The jury sought an alternate, demurred, and debated. Charles returned to look at the Hartley picture several times and finally declared that it was the best in the show and that "as far as I'm concerned, that's it." That the painting was then voted a special honorable mention—in view of the fact that the money was but an earthly symbol, as far as Hartley then was concerned—was as much a tribute to the aesthetic integrity of Charles as to the quality of Hartley painting itself.

I forget precisely when I next saw the Sheelers. A reminiscence is for remembering, not for forgetting. It could have been three or four times at the Downtown Gallery in New York where Edith Gregor Halpert had long exhibited his work, or perhaps, at a museum function or two. His work had not been unknown to me, however, because Constance Rourke had visited the Addison Gallery a short time after her biography of him was published, and I had then become very much aware of the quality of his vision.

107 Reflection 1946

81 City Interior #2 1935

II

A small museum on a preparatory school campus, such as the Addison Gallery at Phillips Academy, cannot expect to represent the work of every American artist, even though it specializes in the field. Furthermore, it probably has no legitimate reason for attempting to do so, as my predecessor, Charles Sawyer, and I had more than once agreed. Toward the end of World War II, as preoccupations with various emergency efforts lessened, I found time for conjectures which had been impossible to dwell on before. One was to ask myself whether the medieval church and the Renaissance court possessed a better opportunity for aesthetic encouragement of the artists who served them—and, in turn, whom they served to benefit through their patronage—than pertains in the 20th century. I wondered if greater meaning might be discovered

140 Ore into Iron 1953

165 Continuity 1957

by seeking a similar relationship between the museum and the contemporary artist. It then occurred to me that the sort of person with whom I might enjoy exploring such a question could be my friend Charles Sheeler. To have gone to him directly would have been possible, but there is a third party to the present-day encouragement of both artist and collector who, when performing best, is something like an aesthetic priest. Frequently denoted by the title, dealer, this minister of the artistic faith is one whom I wished to include in any such conversation. Accordingly, Edith Halpert, who had for many years performed those rites for Charles, and I drove to the Sheelers' "Birdsnest" one pleasant spring Sunday in 1946.

"Birdsnest" is a small two-story, granite treasure-box which once was the gatekeeper's lodge of a large estate overlooking the Hudson at Irvington, New York. The mansion itself had been destroyed. The land, the huge sculptural beech trees, and the slate mansard-roof of the cottage were visual clues to the grandeur of the mansion, which itself once gave stature to the surroundings. I was to learn in succeeding years that it was Charles and Musya Sheeler who now gave the lodge stature. Its simple elegance suited them both, and they graced it.

After the greetings were completed and as the so-called preliminaries were cooled and sipped, whilst a steak was grilling in the budding yard outdoors, I posed my question:

"Charles, would you rather know for whom you are painting? Or would you rather paint for yourself and then toss the picture to the breeze, so to speak?"

I don't recall his exact reply, but the gist of it was that he was accustomed to trust the disposal of his work to Edith and, because she was an attractive breeze, he didn't consider *that* to be random tossing. Charles had a dry, almost innocent wit, sometimes misunderstood, with which he often articulated serious matters. But more of that later, for it is to be discerned in his art. Edith was familiar with his mode of conversation and merely grinned by way of acknowledgment. Charles went on, as if he hadn't himself noticed what he had said (a characteristic habit), to point out that from time to time he had been engaged in fulfilling specific commissions, but that he accepted them only when he felt agreeable both to the assignment and the person offering it, otherwise he would rather work alone.

I pursued my own point further and said:

"From time to time I have wondered about our normal museum policy of acquiring an example of the work of an artist (whom we may or may not know) which in a sense is merely objectively regarded because it has no special relevance to the museum or its community. On the other hand, I grant that it may subjectively reveal something about our contemporary environment. Might it be possible to increase the subjective interest by finding a work which could be related to the particular area of the museum more intimately?"

He teased me with a typical twinkling eye: "You're rooting for local artists?"

"Not to deny them," I replied, catching his twinkle, and yet taking his words seriously. "I would like to find a way to establish a relationship between the Addison Gallery and an artist in whose work we believe rather than merely to acquire some-

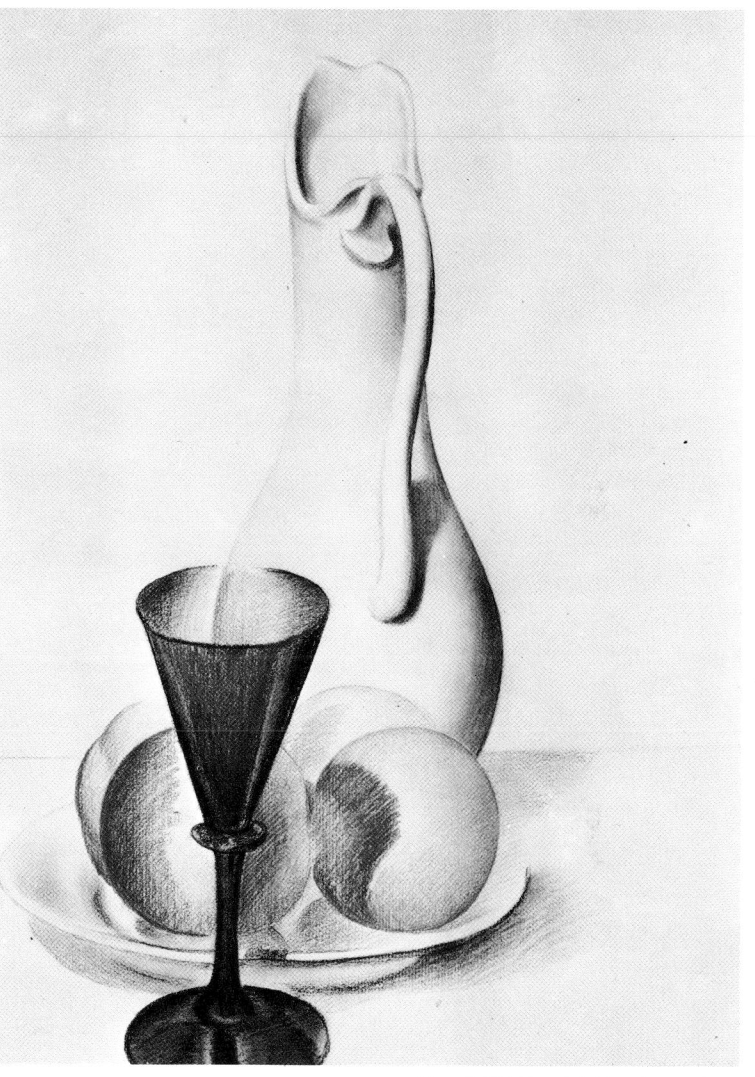

30 Still Life with Peaches 1923

thing which has no personal association—in other words, to create a meaningful bond between the artist, his work, and the museum. If we could do this from time to time, it might provide the collection of the Addison Gallery of American Art with a greater interest than could otherwise be possible."

He replied with a deep-throated, noncommittal sound which I have heard many times since and learned to recognize as an audible signal that he was thinking. There may be a better written indication for it, but "uh-huh" will do.

He waited for me to expand my point. "Specifically," I said, "if instead of going to Edith and selecting a work which you have tossed to your Breeze (I had learned in Chicago to return his banter, a fact which, now that I think of it, may have established a rapport between us at the outset), we should invite you to Andover as a complete family—Ebony, your dachshund, as well as Musya—to live in our community for a period of time, so that you learn to know it—literally uproot you, paying your living costs. Would this appeal to you, and would you be willing, in return for this, to allow us the privilege to select any painting which would result from your experience? Wouldn't that painting have more meaning both for you and the Museum?" As an afterthought I added, "We would select the painting for a consideration, of course."

Again his short humor: "I like the consideration the best."

He went to look at the steak, and upon returning asked, "How long a time are you thinking of uprooting us? We're kind of attached to our Birdsnest here."

I fumbled for a reply, for indeed he had a point. "Well, it could be a school year, a term of three months, or even a shorter time. I have no set plan—enough, perhaps to let you feel that you have become a member of the community."

It was an important part of Charles' personality that there were times when banter would not serve his purpose. He replied almost laconically, "Well, we'll think about it." It was like closing up the desk and going out to lunch. It was time, for the steak was ready.

III

The initial stay at Andover the following autumn lasted, in fact, little more than a month, but there were to be visits in later years which refreshed our friendship and reinforced the local influences which in certain respects seemed to have formed a turning point in his career.

For one thing, his use of color suddenly became vigorous, almost violent. Whether this was because of the brilliance of the autumn forest, or the rapid pace of campus events of which he became a natural part (an experience new to him), or whether it was the social kaleidoscope of students and faculty which confronted him is hard to say—possibly all three. He was never one to avoid people, as best I can tell; on the other hand, a campus life involves one with many people, constantly, not merely a few friends for dinner or an occasional large party which is common to off-campus life. There is a continuous interweaving of personalities, yet because personalities are

170 Composition around White 1959

122 Wings 1949

what they are, there are also strong contrasts. In short, his life was active (although he never actually taught), so much so that he had to drive off into the surrounding country to find time to think—to think and to react to the environment. I had expected him to respond to the Phillips Academy campus itself, to the school buildings, the sports, the elm-divided extent of lawn, but apart from a few photographs and an occasional sketch of these elements of the school there seemed to be too much action for him to fix it consciously and turn it to his own use. His responses were subtler. The very escape from the campus activity—which driving in the environs provided—seems to have made the relative calm all the more impressionable. At all events, this dichotomy between active and passive is what I read into the painting *Ballardvale* [no. 106, illustrated], which was eventually selected for the Addison Gallery "for a consideration."

Ballardvale is a manufacturing hamlet, a subdivision of Andover. It is literally a vale, named for a resident named Ballard, wherein factory buildings nestle along the winding Shawsheen River, which provided water power at the beginning of the industrial revolution. Some of the first locomotives to be built in America were con-

98 The Artist Looks at Nature 1943

structed there when the local railroad was laid in 1836. Gas lighting equipment was made there when gas became the accepted mode of illumination. And, of course, textile entrepreneurs, the one-time base of the New England economy, erected their structures too. Charles was intrigued with the history and with its dramatic remains, for the shuttles of the flannel mill long had lain still. Now the gaunt chimney rises silently (one could almost hear the smoke that poured skyward when the factory was alive). The red brick sheds are bare, except where green moss clings to them in the dampness of the river. But for occasional freshets, even the stream has slowed to a trickle over the dam: *Reflection* [no. 107, illustrated]. The physical specter of the past thrusts itself into the vivid autumn sky, carrying with it something of its tombstone essence, as the factory vapors once distilled its purposeful strength. The painting is a transcript, not a photograph of the original factory, and its austere character is in some way a fusion of the strength of the antique and the campus activity to which he returned from the vale.

Andover appears to have been a turning point in his art, not only in terms of crisply interlocking form and color, but also in another new direction. The exposure to and the virtual immersion in what might be described today as Andover's "psychedelic" activities (in the sense that multiple impressions impinge on one simultaneously from all sides, so much movement is there) may account for his shift in outlook, for certainly there was a shift. His earlier paintings are seen from a fixed point of view as definite objects, or scenes; his later ones are complex visions of a host of interrelated observations. His interiors, for example, painted before 1946, either are different views of the same interior or of different interiors. His factory landscapes, although selectively simplified, are observed from a fixed vantage point in the sense of Renaissance perspective. Contrast any of them—*City Interior #2* [no. 81, illustrated] will do—with later industrial paintings, such as *Ore into Iron* [no. 140, illustrated] or *Continuity* [no. 165, illustrated]. His still lifes illustrate his response to the traditional perspective training under William Chase modified by his respect for the avant-garde paintings he saw in Paris in 1909, which he didn't understand, he said, but felt, nevertheless, that the painters knew what they were doing.

Still Life with Peaches [no. 30, illustrated] most likely was influenced by his admiration for Cezanne. In an interview with William Lane in 1958, he describes a small Cezanne still life which was lent to him by Walter Arensberg while Charles was working in the De Zayas Gallery in New York.

"That picture was painted by one of the Angels," he is recorded. There is a pause, and then he adds, "Incredible!"

Sheeler's still life reveals the form of the pitcher seen through the wine glass before it. The rim of the glass virtually disappears at this point. A photograph would doubtless reveal the rim more clearly, as it would the curving right edge of the plate. Although he was an artist with the camera, he was another artist when painting or drawing. His ability to see through and around things, nevertheless, anticipates his later omniscient vision, but he is rooted in his earlier training at this stage in his development.

Even the abstract barn drawn in 1917 [no. 15, illustrated, page 35] describes an

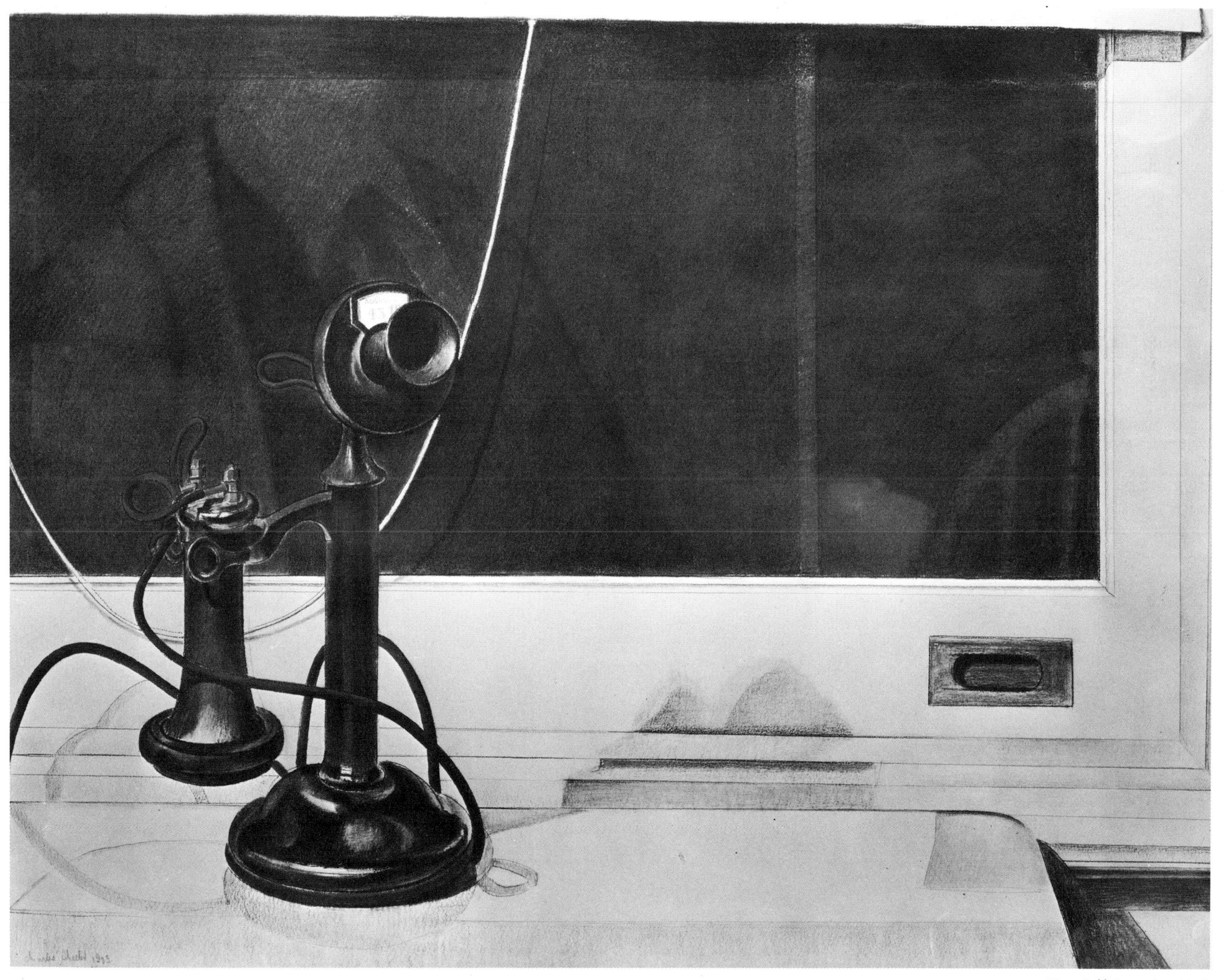

32 Self Portrait 1923

67 Interior with Stove 1932

actual barn viewed from a particular spot, by contrast with similar themes painted after his Andover residence, such as *Composition around Red (Pennsylvania)* [no. 167], *Composition around White* [no. 170, illustrated], and *On a Connecticut Theme* [no. 166], wherein the images are derived from moving around and through the setting. The very titles define the manipulative process.

The abstracted views of New York City skyscrapers, which were painted after he made his documentary film of them in cooperation with Paul Strand in 1920, also are seen to be no more than sensitive simplifications observed from a particular angle. Indeed, the film itself possesses a single perspective quality despite its movement. The camera swings from a fixed pivot, then changes to another. People, cars, and even boats move objectively within an established projected image. One of the most abstract of these early city paintings, *Church Street El,* 1920 [no. 24, illustrated, page 39], recalls the oblique essence of the film *Manhatta.* Accenting the extremes of sunlight and shadow, it is an abstraction of a typical frame from that cinematic, yet static, series of images as well as an abstraction of that particular urban place. It is, as are all his paintings over the years, a reinterpretation. Like the film, its viewpoint is directed from a specific direction; like the film, another image derived from another position was to be another painting. After the Andover sojourn, his paintings synthesize various observations in space and time in a single painting.

If an exception can be cited to prove the thesis that Andover was a turning point and that an artist working freely, independently, yet purposefully, knowing the kind of environment that his work will inhabit is thereby especially benefited by being stimulated to alter his sights, I should look with special care at three earlier phases of Charles' work, to see if they are, in truth, exceptions.

The first phase includes those paintings which follow the 1913 Armory show. I have in mind, especially, an abstract landscape, painted in 1915 [no. 10, illustrated, page 33], now in the collection of William Lane. One can argue that the way Charles has composed the subject involves different aspects of the actual landscape seen from a variety of frontal views. I have a sense, rather, that the composition results from an analysis of voids and masses—the tangible elements such as trees, houses, and the like—linked to the intangible spaces between them which are symbolized as shapes, but that, as with his other pre-Andover observations, these are conceived from a single, monocular position.

Be that as it may, the second seeming exception is the painting *Pertaining to Yachts and Yachting,* dated 1922 [no. 28, illustrated, page 46]. Granted that the sails overlap in a manner suggestive of his multiperspective later work, it must be obvious that this overlapping is precisely what a camera would reveal from a single point of view. A quick glance at *Wings,* 1949 [no. 122, illustrated], will disclose the difference in his later vision and subsequent interpretation of the changing world.

The world was, and indeed still is, changing with increasing swiftness. Concrete straps buckle together communities which a century ago would have had little to do with one another. Consumer goods, as well as producer goods, which once were local—generating local pride and atmosphere—are now international. From the ap-

13 Lhasa 1916

pearance of airport architecture, it is literally impossible to say if one is in London, Tokyo, Rio de Janeiro, or Cairo, except for the predominance of the native language. The point is that Andover was only incidental to the kind of fresh discernment which developed in Charles. The kind of campus activity and the environment I have alluded to has been organically evolving around the globe. The astronauts have sensed it in a matter of 17 minutes. Nevertheless, the Andover environment seems to have pin-pointed Charles' own awareness of it.

The third possible exception was painted three years prior to his first Andover visit and is, to the best of my knowledge, unique in character. I refer to *The Artist Looks at Nature* [no. 98, illustrated]. As a self-portrait, it is a good likeness, even though viewed from behind, and is far more specific that the earlier *Self Portrait* [no. 32, illustrated], where the telephone commands attention and only as an after-image is the artist discovered reflected from chin to waist in the window. Charles was fond of paradoxes which gratified his trenchant humor, to which I have already referred. The drawing is one of them, and it is distinctly singular rather than multiple as an observed

120 Ballardvale Revisited 1949

image despite the reflection. The later portrait, however, is composed of things seen at different times and typifies the time-space relationships of his later, more exploratory investigations and work. On the other hand, the various objects represented are recognized as objective symbols rather than the subjective shapes of which most of his post-Andover work is comprised. For example, the interior on the easel is a recall of an earlier interest, *Interior with Stove* [no. 67, illustrated]. The ramparts and flights of stairs, probably a reference to *Lhasa* [no. 13, illustrated] are observed by his own present self in retrospect, objectively pieced together as the rational mind pieces such things, but not the visionary mind which he exercised to a more incisive degree later on. Here again in this painting is a love of paradox where he himself plays the central role. He is presumably copying an exterior view, but an interior appears before him. Both images involve substantive things and man's mastery of them. Although not a church-goer, he was a religious man in his adoration of the human spirit and the natural world in which it flourishes if nature is well attended. Charles, the artist, metaphorically reconciles the external body with his internal ponderings.

Charles did ponder. On the campus at Andover and in his meanderings there was no easel (the easel in the painting is a witticism). After he looked and looked, however, he thought, composed, and recomposed. One summer, on a later visit, it became terribly hot. I came home one noon to find Musya alone with my wife.

"Where is Charles?" I asked. She replied that he was in the coal cellar. He was there, perched on a sawhorse in the dim, dusty light.

"What in the world?" I asked.

"Gee, it's great down here," he replied. "I can't stand that heat upstairs."

"Well, are you cooled off now? Why don't you come up to have lunch?"

He didn't budge.

I tried another tack, "What have you been thinking about?"

"I dunno."

He needed these intervals of solitude, and didn't emerge until dusk.

His return visits to Andover had something in them of the multiple-image style and philosophy which, subconsciously perhaps, was in the process of his discovery during his first visit. Having painted *Ballardvale,* not while at Andover but upon his return to Irvington, after much introspection, he did not abandon it and turn elsewhere. He visited it again both in person and in imagination, as the title of another painting, *Ballardvale Revisited* [no. 120, illustrated], testifies. Indeed, multiple images appear frequently in the work done after Andover, and the several paintings on any particular theme are variations of it, interconnected yet individual; he was beginning to paint anew, in a space-time context, not only symbolically, as in *The Artist Looks at Nature,* but visually.

There are some who have tended to confuse his interest in photography with his interest in painting, believing that the latter was merely a reproduction of the former. Evidence to the contrary is amply demonstrated in the Ballardvale series. If a photograph were used to touch the memory [photograph, illustrated], it was no more a determinant of the painting than a sketch, or memory itself. A comparison of *Counter-*

Photograph by Charles Sheeler of a mill in Ballardvale, Massachusetts (not exhibited)

118 Counterpoint 1949

111 Architectural Planes 1947

point and *Architectural Planes* [nos. 118, 111, illustrated], along with others already mentioned, should be convincing enough that his introspection as a painter extended as far from the photograph as it did from the physical source, the red brick mill.

The Andover adventure was the cause of an invitation similar to the Addison program, from Gordon Smith, then director of the Currier Gallery in nearby Manchester, New Hampshire. Some of the paintings Charles did there are less evocative than the Ballardvale series—rather more factual, but also more competent and intricate; *Amoskeag Canal* and *Manchester* [nos. 114, 117, illustrated]. Ultimately the two experiences became fused, as seen in *New England Irrelevancies* [no. 139, illustrated]. He had found a way to combine his sense of the single image with his search for the many. He had found a way to develop his sketch of whatever the concept might be, refining its form on illustration board until the spatial relationships were outlined—as if on a blue print—sufficiently to satisfy the artistic mood in process of expression. Painting then on glass—subsequently on clear plastic—a material suggested to him by William Lane—he would lay his color and value studies over his "blueprint" until he had discovered a meaningful solution, combining and recombining the composition as nature herself has eternally done. The "unnaturalness" of his latest work notwithstanding, Charles was about as close to nature and her way of working as any artist has been. He was pulling his world together.

IV

The entire story of his life is not my part to tell. Excellent biographies exist: among them the study by Constance Rourke, 1938; later, by Frederick Wight, in the catalogue of the Sheeler survey at the University of California, Los Angeles, 1954; and, still more recently, in an essay by Lillian Dochterman for the exhibit catalogue of a similar survey at the University of Iowa, 1963, two years before his death. He was then an invalid. The artistic story was complete. There were to be no more paintings. But his spirit continued, as did his conversation and his joy in banter and make-believe. My wife and I had given him a small, white poodle, although he had asserted that he would never own another pet following the deaths of his earlier ones. Upon contemplating her fluffy whiteness, he agreed to let her stay for awhile. He accepted her and named her Vanilla for, as he put it, "If I'm going to have a white dog around the house, make mine Vanilla." As the months wore on, Vanilla became his constant companion, as close as the white hairs on his own head. He would refer to her as the Princess of the Universe and meant every word of it. And he ought to have known.

Charles Sheeler had many friends, many who could and still can recount anecdotes illuminating different sides of his personality and artistic bias. His wife, Musya, still relates an intriguing variety of them. One whom he most admired was William Carlos Williams, physician and poet. I met Dr. Williams at "Birdsnest" only once, but Charles spoke of him often. They had in common a love of the dignity of man and of his existence as a humble yet inspired product of nature. A copy of the

117 Manchester 1949

114 Amoskeag Canal 1948

Autobiography of William Carlos Williams, inscribed to Charles and Musya Sheeler, October 7th, 1951, has been deposited at Charles' wish in the rare book section of the Oliver Wendell Holmes Library at Phillips Academy, for it was there, as well as elsewhere on the Andover campus, that Charles Sheeler felt at home. It seems appropriate to excerpt from it:

Until we have reorganized the basis of our thinking in any category, we cannot understand our errors. An advance of estimable proportions is made by looking at poems as a field, rather than an assembly of more or less ankylosed lines. . . . In presenting the reconstruction of the poem as one of the major occupations of the intelligence in our day, take the following example:

After nine years Charles Sheeler had married again. His bride was Musya Sokolova, a dancer who at the age of fifteen had been driven from Russia by the Revolutionists.

*He abandoned the place at Ridgefield where he had taken her, and came to live in the Hudson River valley near New York. He had got hold of the gardener's cottage of the former Lowe estate, a miniature mansion of grey stone, mansard-roof style, deep-set French windows that was perfect to his purpose . . . . Charles Sheeler, artist, has taken the one rare object remaining more or less intact . . . a stone unit of real merit stylistically and proceeded to live in it . . . and make a poem (a painting of it) . . . . It is ourselves we organize in this way not against the past or for the future or even for survival but for integrity of understanding to insure persistence, to give the mind its stay. The poem (in Charles' case the painting) is the construction in understandable limits of his life . . . . That is a feat of the intelligence . . . to transfer values into a new context, to make a poem again.**

15 April 1968 BARTLETT HAYES

---

* From *The Autobiography of William Carlos Williams*. Copyright © by William Carlos Williams 1951. Reprinted by permission of New Directions Publishing Corporation.

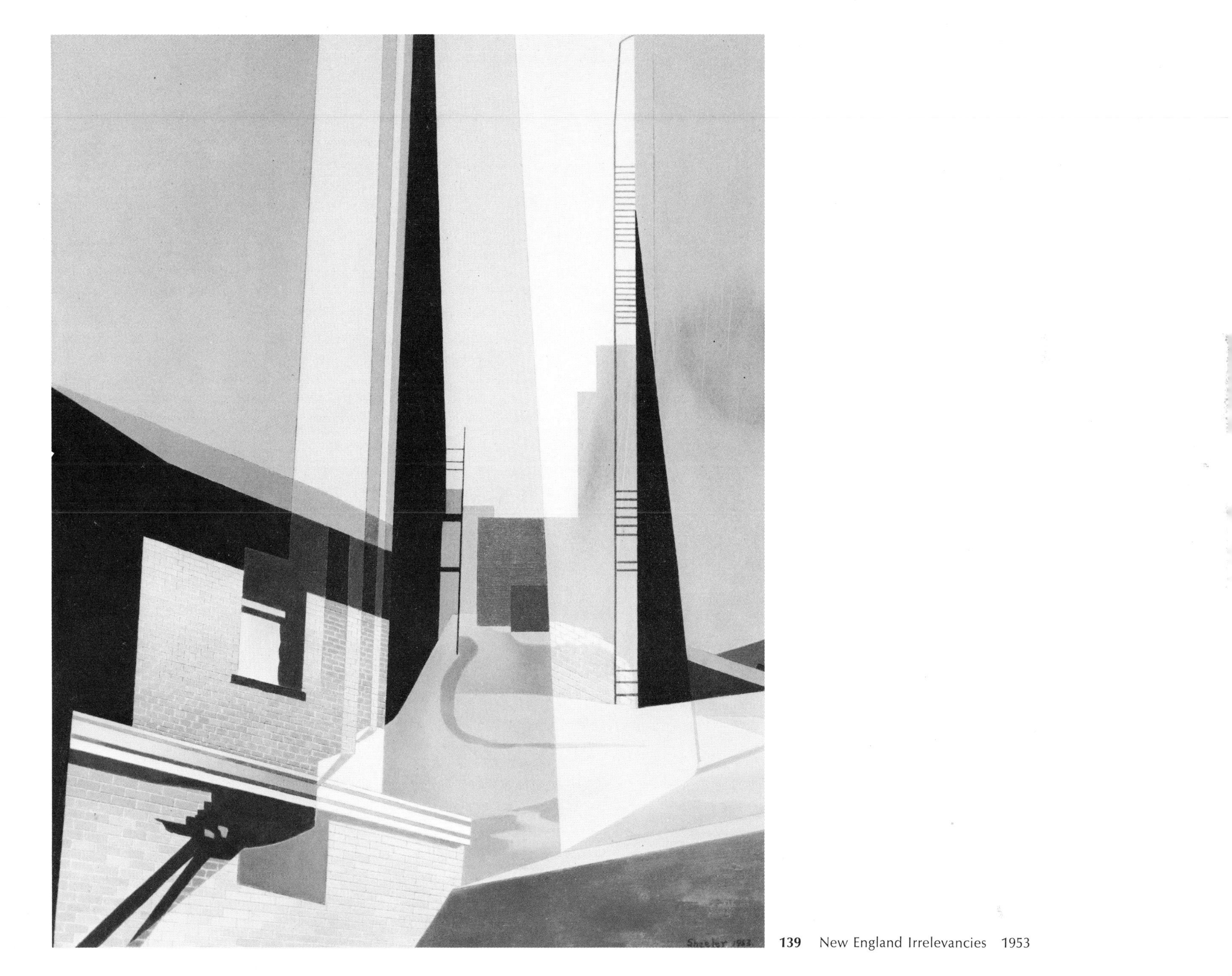

139 New England Irrelevancies 1953

12 Pennsylvania Barn 1915

Photography has the capacity for accounting for things seen in the visual world with an exactitude for their differences which no other medium can approximate.—CHARLES SHEELER.

THE PHOTOGRAPHY OF CHARLES SHEELER

Forty-five years have passed since Henry McBride described Charles Sheeler's *Side of a White Barn* [titled *Pennsylvania Barn* in this exhibition, no. 12, illustrated] as "one of the most noteworthy productions in the history of photography" and since Sheeler himself was intimately connected with the most significant formative talents in the history of American photography—Alfred Stieglitz, Paul Strand, Edward Steichen, Edward Weston, and Ansel Adams. In those years, Sheeler's photography has almost completely disappeared from public view. Few photographers are now aware that Sheeler was other than a painter or that his photographs were once considered revolutionary in both vision and quality. This is due partly to the fact that, as with everything revolutionary, what once seemed innovative is now commonplace. Sheeler's "straight," unsentimentalized, sharply focused pictures of urban and industrial life, so remarkable in an era steeped in pictorialism, helped shape the vision on which almost all the best contemporary photography is based. Now that Sheeler's photographs fit into an accepted visual convention, they attract attention less easily than they did, and since Sheeler's sensibility was extremely reticent and his pictures lack the monumentality and drama of the work of, say, Stieglitz, Weston, or Adams, the photographs can easily be overlooked when their novelty has worn off.

Equally important as a factor in the neglect of Sheeler's photography were his own attitudes. Increasingly, Sheeler de-emphasized photography in favor of painting. He seldom tried to sell his photographs and never taught photography or was associated with any organization in the field. He last allowed his photographs to be exhibited at a commercial gallery in 1931, although important museum shows included his photographic work in 1939 and 1954. Nor were Sheeler's photographs widely published after the early 30s. Those that were resulted from the commissions with which Sheeler helped support himself or were concessions to friends—as when, in the early 40s, Edward Weston used a Sheeler photograph as one of the few to illustrate his article on photography for *Encyclopaedia Brittanica*. Although his work progressively disappeared from public view, Sheeler never ceased taking photographs for their own sake, nor has the passage of time tarnished the inherent quality of his photography, that basic strength on which its reputation and importance will ultimately rest.

Charles Sheeler first took up photography in 1912 at the age of 29. Having finished his painting studies with William Merritt Chase, he soon discovered that he could not support himself as a painter and, casting around for a source of income that would in some way relate to his chosen vocation, he determined on photography

16 African Mask 1917

This essay is basically an abridgment of material gathered for an issue of the magazine *Contemporary Photographer* devoted exclusively to Charles Sheeler's photography. Since full documentation is to be found in that article, in the interests of continuity all footnotes and source references are omitted here.

50 River Rouge Plant—Slag Buggy 1927

and trained himself in its technique. His first work was for Philadelphia architects, making records of their work and supplying them with pictures for portfolios to be shown to prospective clients. During the two years which were occupied with this work, Sheeler spent a good deal of time in New York, gradually becoming involved with the circle of avant-garde artists and collectors centered around Alfred Stieglitz and his 291 gallery. Through contacts made on these trips, Sheeler began photographing works of art for dealers, such as Parish-Watson and Knoedler, and private collectors such as Albert Barnes. By 1914 he had given up architectural photography altogether for this more lucrative work.

In 1915, Sheeler's friend Marius De Zayas opened a New York gallery, and throughout 1916 he employed Sheeler extensively to photograph his stock. In 1917, De Zayas published a portfolio of Sheeler photographs of African sculpture in his collection, the work which first drew general attention to Sheeler's photography, and in the same year De Zayas twice showed photographs by Sheeler in his gallery. In 1919, Sheeler moved from Philadelphia to New York, and the following year he began to work for De Zayas, managing the gallery when its owner was away. This arrangement continued until 1923 when the gallery closed.

Luckily for Sheeler, the closing of De Zayas' gallery and the consequent curtailment of his income was closely followed by an invitation from Edward Steichen—then head of photography for Condé Nast Publications—to make fashion and portrait pictures for *Vogue* and *Vanity Fair*. This studio work lasted until 1929. During the same period, Sheeler developed a flourishing business in free-lance advertising photography, which helped support him through the early years of the Depression. His most important client was the advertising firm of N. W. Ayer and Son of Philadelphia, an association that was to bring him the most important commission of his photographic career. In 1927 Sheeler was sent to photograph the Ford Motor Company's River Rouge plant by Vaughan Flannery, art director of N. W. Ayer, who had persuaded Ford that it should have a photographic record of its operations to serve as a permanent document of contemporary American industry. Sheeler spent six weeks at River Rouge, studied his subject carefully, and took 32 photographs. These pictures drew wide public and professional attention almost immediately. They were published in several periodicals in the United States, as well as in Europe and Asia. Five years after taking the Ford pictures Sheeler used four of them to create a photomural triptych for the Museum of Modern Art's 1932 exhibition *Murals by American Painters and Photographers,* which was intended to suggest mural projects to the architects of Rockefeller Center. The center panel of Sheeler's triptych was an overprinting of two separate negatives, resulting in the double-exposure effect that he was to exploit much later in his painting.

In 1932 Sheeler gave up commercial photography, which had kept him solvent, and returned to painting almost full time. During the 30s, he worked on no photographic commissions as such, although he often made extensive photographic studies for painting commissions to be executed in his studio. With the onset of World War II, however, Sheeler foresaw a drop in the demand for his paintings and accepted the invitation of Francis Henry Taylor, director of the Metropolitan Museum, to take a position photographing the Museum's treasures, which were being put into storage for the duration of the war. Since the Museum was also expanding its program of publications and needed photographs for that purpose, Sheeler's pictures were used for the Museum's *Bulletin* as well as for its various other publications. Sheeler's first color work was done for *Bulletin* covers, and the influence of this experience may be seen in the heightened color in his painting after he left the Museum in 1945. During the period he worked for the Metropolitan, Sheeler took on one other photographic commission: two still-life compositions in the style of 19th-century painting for a *Fortune* magazine series, "Americans Whose Careers Are Relevant Today." His subjects were Thoreau and Whitman.

After the war, Sheeler continued to pursue photography with vigor, although he had no further involvement with commercial photography and the photographs he took were largely kept to himself. As in the 30s, he frequently made photographic studies for commissioned paintings that he wished to execute in his studio. From 1959, when he suffered an incapacitating stroke, until his death in 1965 Sheeler's photographic activity was restricted to supervising his wife in printing some of his pictures.

Although his work in commercial photography helped sharpen Sheeler's photographic vision and technique, as well as providing him with a livelihood, few of his best creative efforts resulted from it. Among the African and Ford pictures are some that can be ranked with the best of his independent work, but in general he seems to have confined himself in commissioned work to producing an acceptable, workmanlike product. His portraits for *Vogue*, for instance, although they sometimes surpass Steichen's in abstract compositional force, never match his fellow photographer's work in evocation of personality. Perhaps the most important result of Sheeler's commercial work was that it often required him to produce groups of pictures of the same or similar subjects, a habit he carried over into his independent work in the creation of several series of pictures which he thought of as collective portraits of the subjects involved. In general, however, he struggled to free himself from the demands of commercial photography, and did so whenever it was financially feasible.

Toward the end of his early efforts as an architectural photographer, Sheeler took the first of his independently creative pictures. Although they may be seen as related to the architectural photographs, since they are interiors of the Doylestown house he shared with Morton Livingston Schamberg, these pictures are entirely different in concept. They are strongly lighted close-ups of interior details in which the sharp patterns of light and dark combine with shallow depth to create strong surface patterns of considerable abstract force. Taken in 1914, they perhaps reflect Sheeler's growing knowledge of, and interest in, avant-garde (particularly Cubist) painting, evidenced by his participation in the Armory Show of the previous year.

The final series of twelve photographs of the Doylestown house first attracted Stieglitz to Sheeler's photography. They were also to be the subjects of Sheeler's first

11 Stairwell 1915

25 New York circa 1920

one-man show, held by De Zayas in 1917. One of them, a picture of a window, won Sheeler the $100 first prize at the 1918 photography exhibition held by Wanamaker's in Philadelphia, the jury for which included Stieglitz and Arthur Carles. During this period Sheeler was also doing some still-life photography, as well as taking pictures of barns in the Bucks County countryside. Among these is *Side of a White Barn*, one of his best known photographs. By 1918, only six years after he had taken up photography, Sheeler's photographs had attracted sufficient attention to cause a Philadelphia critic to mention him as one of "*the* Trinity of Photography," the others being Paul Strand and Schamberg.

After his move to New York in 1919, Sheeler was engaged in two closely related photographic projects that brought him further professional and public attention. One was a six-minute movie evocation of New York, made with Paul Strand, which included titles from Walt Whitman and was called *Manhatta*. After a week's showing in New York in 1921, *Manhatta* was chosen along with works by Apollinaire and Satie for an avant-garde program in Paris. Sheeler's other project was a series of still photographs of the city, mostly pictures of midtown buildings seen at a sharp downward angle. Sheeler again used the structural relationships of the buildings and the play of shadow and light to create surface pattern. For Edward Weston, who saw the New York pictures on his first trip to the city in 1922, these were "the finest architectural photographs I have seen," and "had a genuine grandeur—nobility."

During the period of his commercial work in the 20s, Sheeler took few photographs purely for personal satisfaction. Notable among those few are a series of nudes made about 1922 and a few portraits of friends. This choice of subject was, again, related to the commercial, in this case, figure work in which he was engaged. As soon as he was released from the demands of commercial work, Sheeler returned immediately to taking pictures to please himself. On a trip to Europe in 1929 to see the German exhibition *Film und Foto* in which he was exhibiting, he took a series of 14 pictures of Chartres cathedral which are among the very finest of his work, and of which he himself was extremely fond. After the European trip, and with his increasing absorption in painting, Sheeler seems at last to have found a way to integrate his deep commitment to creative photography with the demands of painting and supporting himself. Whereas previously his best photographic efforts had been independent and his commercial work tended to be of lower quality, during the 30s and 40s Sheeler's best pictures were those made as studies for commissioned paintings. In 1935 and 1936, for instance, he spent time in Williamsburg making studies for the paintings now in the Williamsburg Inn. Out of this series came the beautiful photograph *Williamsburg Stairwell* [titled *Stairway* in this exhibition, no. 77, illustrated]. Three years later he made a series of industrial photographs as notes for six paintings on the subject "Power" commissioned by *Fortune* magazine. One of his finest photographs, a picture of a locomotive called *Wheels*, was part of this series. This was the picture chosen by Sheeler to be included in Weston's article in *Encyclopaedia Britannica*, and, indeed, was closely imitated by Weston himself in a picture of 1941 called *Santa Fe 4-8-4*. Other outstanding photographs from the same series included pictures of Boulder Dam and the TVA power project at Guntersville, Alabama. Certain of his assignments for the Metropolitan Museum seem also to have been extremely congenial to Sheeler, and his photographs of the Museum's Assyrian reliefs are among his best work.

Among the best pictures of the last decade of Sheeler's creative life are those taken when he was making painting studies, notably a photograph of storage tanks [no. 135, illustrated] taken in conjunction with a painting commissioned in 1952 by the Meta-Mold Aluminum Company. Architectural photography was again rewarding for Sheeler, most notably in pictures of Rockefeller Center, the United Nations, and Lever House. He also made most of his few photographic nature studies during this time. These included photographs made in Sequoia and Yosemite National Parks, and a series of details of a beech tree in the side yard of his home at Irvington, New York.

The independent creative photography on which Sheeler's claim to importance as a photographer rests embodied a vision uniquely his own. Although his pictures shared a "straight," sharp-focused, uncropped quality with the work of other important photographers of his time, Sheeler's photographs are differentiated from those of his contemporaries by their lack of dramatic assertiveness and by their tendency toward surface composition, a tendency which evidences Sheeler's awareness of trends in contemporary painting. Sheeler did not use light and dark contrast to dramatize his subjects, but rather for the abstract two-dimensional cohesiveness the resulting patterns gave his pictures. He was a master of subtle gradations of tonality, which gives some of his best work a unifying silvery cast of extreme delicacy. In his earlier work, notably the African pictures, Sheeler sometimes used sepia toning to achieve the unity of effect he later produced by these gradations of gray.

The subjects of his best pictures were almost always overtly structural, often architectural, which tends to give an underlying tautness to his evanescent surface effects. To increase this tautness Sheeler abstracted his subjects by composing them "without setting, foreground plane, environment, or identifying intermediaries, thus removing [them] the more from emotional response." The resulting nonassociational quality, combined with Sheeler's straight photographic technique, was what so impressed the Stieglitz group. It led Edward Steichen to remark that "Sheeler was objective before the rest of us were." Combined with the emotional force with which Sheeler invested his photographs, it is also the basis of their continuing appeal.

The relationship between photography and painting in Sheeler's work is subtle and easily misunderstood. Because his paintings were so precise and superficially "photographic," it is easy to jump to the conclusion that they depended wholly on, and were an extension of, his photographs. Nothing could be further from the truth. Photography and painting were for Sheeler distinct expressive media, each with its own advantages and limitations and each appropriate to the solution of separate problems. He always considered himself primarily a painter, and sought recognition in that field, but as early as 1914 he realized that photography was to be for him a useful expressive medium and recognized that the creative intensity that went into his independent photographs made them closer in quality and intent to

55 Chartres Cathedral 1929

77 Stairway 1935

his painting and drawing than to the commercial photography with which he was forced to support himself. Early in Sheeler's career, when he concentrated on painting, both commercial and creative photography tended to fall by the wayside, but as time went on he was increasingly able to carry on creative photography and painting in conjunction with one another. He did this by using photography as earlier artists had used drawing, to supply notes and studies for paintings. He thus was able to make photographs into which he could put his whole creative being at the same time that he served what he considered his principal art.

This more direct relationship between photography and painting seems to have started in the early 20s, when Sheeler first made paintings and drawings after photographs taken several years earlier. This habit seems to have continued in a desultory way for more than a decade, and one has the impression that Sheeler sometimes stimulated himself toward painting by looking through old photographs and gleaning from them what seemed promising compositions. By the mid 30s, the period of his stay in Williamsburg, he had quite consciously developed the practice of making photographic studies for paintings to be executed in his studio, a practice he followed with every subsequent painting commission. As he explained in conjunction with his *Fortune* magazine painting *Rolling Power*, taken from the photograph *Wheels*, "since I could not camp beside [the locomotive] for the three months I required to paint it, I made a photo." This practice allowed him full creative freedom on the spot, as well as the greatest latitude in the later working out of the painting. In the 50s, Sheeler also developed the habit of making color photographs to have color notes for painted compositions, and Mrs. Sheeler remembers his keeping a slide viewer next to him as he painted to check the colors of scenes he had photographed in other parts of the country.

Beyond this direct use of photographs for painting, it is apparent that certain specific visual effects were suggested to Sheeler by his photography. His attempts at color photography for the Metropolitan Museum were followed closely by more intense colorism in his painting. The overprinted "double-exposure" he made for the Museum of Modern Art triptych seems to have suggested such effects for his painting, and they are common in his later work. Indeed, several photographic prints exist in which Sheeler seems to have been consciously manipulating such effects in the search for a painting composition. One such was taken over for the painting *Ore into Iron*. The way in which light and shade effects are distributed abstractly across the surface of some of his canvases, combining with elements of the subject to create an over-all nonobjective pattern, also recalls his photography, and certain paintings suggest cropped photographic images or the acute upward, downward, or diagonal visual angles that Sheeler obtained with his camera. Ultimately, however, photography served Sheeler in relation to his painting as a fixative for his vision, and its most important place in his work is as a separate but equal expressive medium—a medium of which he was complete master and in which his achievement has been too long neglected.

CHARLES MILLARD

89 Installation 1939

96 Assyrian Relief 1942

126 RCA Building 1950

129 Beech Tree 1951

135 Tanks at Cedarburg 1952

138 Lever Building 1953

160 Two against the White 1957

WRITINGS OF CHARLES SHEELER

Charles Sheeler's writings are as articulate as his paintings, drawings, and photographs —and they show the same rational convictions. Sheeler's statements concerning his art are frequent. He seemed always to have been cordial and cooperative in working with students, critics, and art historians pursuing some inquiry into his work; two lengthy tape-recorded interviews exist, and his views are abundantly available in reliable quotation. The remarkable characteristics of Sheeler's verbal record are its clarity and consistency.

The autobiography (manuscript on Archives of American Art microfilm NSh1), written in 1937 and provided to Constance Rourke for use in preparing her monograph, is a comprehensive discussion of the development of his principles as an artist. Sheeler's statements regarding his art over the succeeding years vary little from those recorded in these two basic texts, even in phrasing. Sheeler's verbal statements, like his art, seem to have been thoroughly explored in his mind, stripped of inessentials, and put forth only when he was absolutely convinced of the expressiveness of their form; therefore, they required little modification and no retraction.

The bibliographic references in this catalogue include sources in which Sheeler discusses Sheeler. In addition to Constance Rourke's book, the reader's attention is drawn particularly to his statements in the catalogues of the Forum exhibition of 1916 and the Museum of Modern Art's retrospective exhibition of 1939.

Three of Sheeler's writings are presented here in their entirety. The two articles originally published in the 20s in *The Arts,* and written by Sheeler in the character of art critic, are thought to provide a special insight to his viewpoint as an artist. The third text, "The Black Book," deserves special explanation.

"The Black Book" was the name given by the Sheelers to a bound notebook in which Sheeler, in the later years of his life, set down some words he felt distilled his ideas as an artist. He prepared it for the use of those who were seriously interested in his art, and it often was shown to researchers and friends. The manuscript, in Sheeler's hand, is reproduced on Archives of American Art microfilm NSh1. The National Collection of Fine Arts is grateful to Mrs. Sheeler for permission to bring "The Black Book" to its deserved destiny—publication.

A. B.

"Recent Photographs by Alfred Stieglitz"

By Charles Sheeler

With the advent of platinum as a basic element in photographic papers, a material preciousness was introduced comparable to the introduction of goldleaf in Italian painting. The cult for platinum prints and the disdain, or at best indulgent tolerance for prints growing out of a less aristocratic element such as silver, reached its apex prior to the war.

Among all of the aspirations toward good that the belligerent nations may have entertained, it is doubtful if any foresaw the reconstructive and creative impulse to

---

Reprinted from *The Arts,* May 1923.

be derived from the enforced acquaintance with new materials, which in some instances succeeded the old and familiar.

That such readjustments are vitally essential to growth was again forcefully evidenced in the recent photographs by Alfred Stieglitz, which were on view last month at the Anderson Galleries. Having achieved the High Renaissance in photography through his earlier platinum prints, conditions outside of his control necessitated experimenting with another medium, the various silver papers, and adapting them to his need. The necessity has introduced new blood, the pulse has been quickened.

In the group of ten photographs of clouds he achieves his highest point of distinction in his last exhibition. Here is most convincingly demonstrated beyond a doubt, that it is within the realm of photography to transcribe and fix eternal qualities. What mingled admiration and anguish would have torn the heart of Albert Ryder in gazing upon these cloud pictures, admiration for the complete expression of a theme ever of profound interest to him, and anguish at the relative inadequacy of his own technical equipment to achieve their equal in his chosen medium.

In one of these photographs there is an area of unmistakable, hard, cold blue expressed with superb intensity. Beneath it a highly sensitive undulating, clear-cut edge of hills for the like of which one must turn to the landscapes of Mantegna. In all of them Stieglitz has succeeded in expressing the transitional forms of clouds so convincingly that one, upon seeing them subsequently, is surprised to find the design remains unchanged.

In turning to the recent portraits which comprise the bulk of the exhibition, one's previous opinion is once more confirmed that the eye of Stieglitz's camera would have been an adjunct of inestimable value at the time of the Inquisition. Sometimes these exhibits A, B [et al.] hover so near the realm of pathology, that so slight a disturbance as the vibration of a passing truck might send them over the borderline. Now our attention is arrested by a head which fills the rectangle to overflowing and presents to us a section of a countenance at such close range that it is as unfamiliar as an astronomical photograph depicting the topography of a distant planet. Again we may be abruptly halted by the portrayal of the tortured, sandaled feet of one who, in order to escape the gruelling [sic], may be confessing to a crime she has never committed. It is the exception when an anguish and internal disquiet, like the creaking doors and strange moanings in a haunted house, do not pervade these portraits. Frequently they achieve a beauty of form relations independent of their human content.

Still another phase of the work of Stieglitz, among the photographs shown, is the recording of buildings and incidents which form a familiar part of his summers at Lake George. Among these, where the human element is a prominent factor, he is happiest. Now and again there reappears a trace of the Munich tradition of painting, as in the barn interior with loaded hay-wagon, the head of an old lady with a lace scarf and kindly smiling face and again in the print of hands holding grapes, as examples. In those photographs which give the most lasting satisfaction, neither time or tradition are suggested, as the two portraits of Marcel Duchamp and the head of a young girl in profile, will forcefully demonstrate.

Recollections of these photographs serve to arouse again the persistent question—how long before photography shall be accorded an importance not less worthy than painting and music as a vehicle for the transmission of ideas? Surely as long as man is the controlling element in the working of the camera, it will be a means of communicating ideas, and with this element as a directing influence, it is evident that the functioning of the camera cannot remain impersonal. No more, in fact, than can the manifestations of the painter's brush or of the musician's instrument.

"Notes on an Exhibition of Greek Art"

By Charles Sheeler

The exhibition of Greek Art on view at the Whitney Studio Galleries gives an excellent opportunity to study the transition from the largely emotional approach of the artists of the Sixth Century B.C., as exemplified in the head of a Core, to the finely adjusted balance of emotion and intellect in the works of the Fourth Century B.C., as the figure of Aphrodite bears witness.

It is of further interest to examine the evidence, as it is beautifully demonstrated in the Aphrodite, that as great purity of plastic expression may be achieved through the medium of objective forms as has been thought to be only obtainable by some of our present day artists, by means of a purely abstract presentation of forms.

The study of abstract problems by pure reason had its origin with the Greeks. Pure speculation in philosophy, as well as in Art, began with them. While developing the mind they also developed the body of man to a high degree of physical perfection. A perfect balance was maintained between the mind and nature, and the means of realizing both of these elements in a single entity was called Art. The Greek miracle was accomplished by the perfect adjustment of concrete form to abstract thought.

In Greek sculpture geometry was the science of form. The knowledge of form was gained and verified by exact observation and correct thinking. Quite different from the geometric art of primitive man, who only conceived form in the imaginary terms of lines and combinations of lines with which he constructs imaginary images addressing themselves to pure feeling, the Art of the Greeks addresses itself to the intelligence as well as to the emotions.

It has been demonstrated convincingly that the Greeks evolved a geometric system of measurements for determining the desired proportions and the relation of the parts to the whole in their sculptures depicting the human figure. The units of measurement varied with the individual work, thereby avoiding the standardization of their Art. It is interesting to note that these geometrical measurements for determining proportions and rhythms are not applicable to Roman copies of Greek sculpture.

Reprinted from *The Arts,* March 1925.

This geometric basis was the internal structure, skillfully concealed, around which was built the objective aspect of nature with all of its sensorial attributes. In our day the attempt to establish this geometric structure at times results in erecting a barrier between the observer and a direct contact and reaction to the combinations of objective forms.

The profound understanding of the harmony of rhythms and proportions enabled the Greek to create sculptures of the smallest dimensions which have the grandeur and scale of works of heroic proportions, as the small Aphrodite and the caryatid well illustrate. So perfectly do the rhythms function that even in a fragment like the section of a figure, the life of the complete conception is not abated.

In the large Aphrodite, it is interesting to observe that the leg supporting the weight of the body, as well as the one in advance, is flexed, giving a beautiful sense of a progression of movement which projects our interest into the future.

Parallel to the intellectual and precise art of the great artists there was in Greece, at all times, an art of pure inspiration which filled a public necessity. It evolved from the fetish to the votive offering and the illustration of life and its caricature. This art frequently offered to the artists who worked in bronze and marble an example, but more often followed the types conceived by the greater artists. It kept its own identity, always evolving but keeping in each period of Greek life a definite character. The great art of sculpture was made of precious materials worthy of the gods to whom it was dedicated. The popular art of the humble koroplasts was made of earth for humans, and if the greater art reveals to us the high mentality of the Greek artist, the figurines reproduce with intensity the dominant characteristics of the contemporary aesthetics.

The Black Book

The miracle of Spring—the first leaf buds and with them the reassurance of life making a new beginning.

The trees in mid-summer with their opulence of celebration.
The unbelievable swan-song of Autumn—the fragrance of burning leaves in the air.
The man-made architecture inlaid in these environments to serve its several purposes.
The look on the faces of human beings in accord with circumstance.
These are among the experiences of artists from which their work derives.

□

Letter to R. F. Piper, Syracuse University

I have your letter with the enclosed form setting forth your project. The title of my picture, "It's a Small World," was probably misleading to you. It could suggest a metaphysical approach to the production of the picture, when as a matter of fact the picture came first and the title followed.

The source of my work in general is the visual world. I try to arrive at an organization of forms which represent my equivalent of the organization I see around me in Nature. There I stop without trying to give expression to any hid[den] or underlying meanings. In a world of conflict and many interpretations I persist in believing that there is always Venus as the symbol of Beauty undisturbed by the transitory.

□

Anticipation or Regret——

The curse upon us is that we may only discern the thing when it is on the horizon—either in advance or retreat—in the moment that we pass the edges are blurred and the form unrecognized.

Painting for me has been a continuous objective pursuit. The pictures I produce are attempts to put down the inherent beauty of the subject with as little personal interference as possible, spoken in a language in general use rather than an exotic one.

I am largely attracted to things seen in nature by instinct for their intrinsic beauty rather than seeing them as manikins upon which to drape my pet theories.

Having no theories I respond to those things which give me a pleasurable reaction, in themselves and their relation to other things, and I attempt to set them down in a visual design.

The resulting work may range from an association of irrelevancies to a combination of forms closely interrelated in function or habit. Neither the identification of natural forms or the absence of identification is essential to establish the value of a picture. The value lies in the degree of satisfaction derived by the Artist and the spectator in the relation of forms set forth within the frame.

□

Paper read at a Symposium on Photography, Museum of Modern Art, 20 October 1950

Do you realize that if all the discussions having to do with the question "Is photography Art?" were laid end to end they would extend from here to—nowhere?

In the meantime photography is promising as a child and there are high hopes for it in its adulthood. Those of us who have been intrigued by acquaintance with a camera are happy to see the application of photography in constantly extended fields. As a means of personal expression it is only limited by the calibre of the operator. The marked progress in optical correction, as well as increased speed, of lenses has in these recent years greatly enlarged our acquaintance with the visual world. Man has produced an eye which in this respect is better than his own. With this and other greatly increased facilities at the disposal of the photographer he is more and more free to move around in the larger world which has been presented to him. With the increase in his vocabulary it is the responsibility as well as the privilege of the photographer to endeavor to extend the field of application.

It is true that increased facilities are not an unmixed blessing, with something gained there is the danger of something lost.

There seems to be a prevalent idea that the sheer weight of numbers is a virtue which with the help of a miracle can only result in better photographs. It is easy to forget that we only take out that which we have put in.

Gone are the days, we hope, when it was thought to be desirable to apologize for photography, being the unique medium that it is, by the dismal failure to disguise it as of the Graphic Arts. There is a tendency to think that painting and photography are converging roads. That photography is an equivalent to a shortcut to painting. This could only bring us back to the Bromoil * which hoped to be a charcoal drawing. Why make the same mistake again when there are so many new ones that can be made.

There is a tendency in current abstract photography to disguise the source— nature —by using unidentifiable forms. This is to encroach upon the field of painting. The searching eye is capable of discovering in Nature a combination of forms which, when recorded and presented in a print, have astonished those who have *missed* the seeing. This can be abstraction, with a credit line to Nature.

All Nature *has* an underlying abstract structure and it is within the province of the artist to search for it and to select and rearrange the forms for the enhancement of his design. It is also within the province of the photographer to seek the same underlying abstract structure and, having found it to his satisfaction, to record it with his camera, with an exactitude not to be achieved through any other medium.

The result is an image which has passed through a lens and having been projected upon a sensitized emulsion makes an inalterable record of the thing seen.

□

Letter

I fail to see the difference in the dilemma of the 20th-century artist and that of any other century. It is true that my personal experience is in the 20th but with some reference to history a comparison may be made.

Within my span I have seen what I consider marked improvements in the relation of the Artist to Society.

In the first place the artist has, in the past considerable number of years, had increasing opportunities of presenting his work to the public. That is certainly one of his principal objectives rather [than] accumulating it in his studio, with a few personal friends for an audience. With the increased publicizing of his work there has also been increased distribution of his work—also a principal objective since no one so far has found a way of subsisting on a diet of pictures. That Art will never be a competitor of TV and baseball in public interest should be readily realized. That which is designated as shapeless and formless by some today may, if History is to repeat itself, become the Classic of tomorrow. This you must have witnessed as well as I.

□

I have been an artist for a considerable time, I hope. On my road-map, from time to time, there have been added a succession of dots, indicating new acquaintances made whom I have come to revere. It is a valued document principally because of these dots.

---

* The Bromoil process, introduced into photography techniques in 1907, was a procedure by which the black-to-white gradations of a photograph were eliminated by bleaching the silver, leaving a shallow relief of colorless gelatin on the photo printing paper. The gelatin would then absorb oil-based pigment applied to the surface with a brush, but the degree of absorption was controlled primarily by the value relationships established in the original photograph. The principal change in the character of the photographic image would be in texture—which would somewhat simulate that of a charcoal or pastel drawing.

Somewhere near the beginning of my career it was a practice to make excursions into the countryside, with a sketch-box, to record in paint the thing seen.

On one of these excursions, seated by the roadside before my subject, I was accosted by a man who, with permission asked, seated himself beside me.

Some would designate him as a tramp, a convenient word for the dismissal of further consideration of him.

His occupation was that of an umbrella mender, a drop of solder on the pot of the farmer's wife, in exchange for a bit of food and lodging for the night in the hayloft. As our conversation developed he quoted passages from Pope's "Essay on Man." Within my knowledge only the author understood it as well.

He also informed me in case I didn't know, and I didn't, that it was an especial experience to sleep among the cattle in an open field and to witness the arrival of a new day. Food must enter into the life of everyone. He had a basket on his arm, bread, tomatoes, scallions, and salt. All with the caress of the sun upon them. He invited me to share with him. It was a privilege.

I do not have a name for him but I like to think of him as Adam. I also like to think of him, as well as the oak, [as] having come out of the earth, and that is reassuring.

□

My work has continuously been based on a clue seen in Nature from which the subject of a picture may be projected.

Nature, with its profound order, is an inexhaustible source of supply. Its many facets lend themselves freely to all who would help themselves for their particular needs.

Each one may filter out for himself that which is essential to him. Our chief objective is to increase our capacity for perception. The degree of accomplishment determines the calibre of the Artist.

Wichita Museum re "Skyline" June 1952

□

It is known that the amoeba is indispensable to the welfare of man. It is a hope that man is indispensable to the welfare of the amoeba.

□

I like to think that operating on alternating current is the only desirable basis.

□

For something received—the offer of one's best in exchange.

□

To a man who knows nothing, Mountains are Mountains, Waters are Waters, and Trees are Trees. But when he has studied and knows a little, Mountains are no longer Mountains, Waters no longer Waters, and Trees no longer Trees. But when he has thoroughly understood, Mountains are again Mountains, Waters are Waters, and Trees are Trees.

Old Zen Saying

I like.

Turkish Proverb.

Before you love
Learn to run through snow
Leaving no footprint

I like.

□

Tagore.

But the truth is, death is not the ultimate reality.
It looks black, as the sky looks blue, but it does not blacken existence just as the sky does not leave its stain upon the wings of the bird.

I believe.

□

[A hand-written letter, clipped into "The Black Book"]

Washington, D. C.
21 October, 1955

Dear Mr. Sheeler,

I am a 12 year old girl and enjoy drawing very much, but with sorrow I see my elders getting nothing out of it anymore.

I am myself afraid of losing that power of conveying my feelings and to you who kept it so well, may I ask:

After coming across a drawing made when you were a very young boy, did you identify it quickly?
What were your feelings?
How did you rate it?

Sincerely yours
M— C—

□

To M— C—
12 years old and having a problem:

I was interested to have your letter and to have you take me into your confidence by telling me of your problem.

Our public does not always keep up to our progress. It is at times discouraging, but if we retain our self-confidence in believing that we are moving toward our objective we can, and do, survive.

Confidence is not to be mistaken for conceit. Confidence in the validity of our objective, even though we never fully achieve it—but in the direction of it.

Don't worry about the loss of your power to convey your feelings as long as you have the desire to convey them. It is to be hoped that, as you progress, you will want to approach your subject in different ways for the fullest expression of it.

It is my constant hope that each picture I produce will in some way be different in my approach to the subject. That is the only way in which I can consider that I have progressed—not by repetition. So don't dwell in the past—live in today and the hope of tomorrow. Yes?

Addressed to Leslie Cheek, Jr.
Virginia Museum of Fine Arts
Richmond, Va.

The subject of my picture Steel-Croton is the bridge at Croton-on-the-Hudson. It had interested me for some time before I decided to organize a picture based upon it.

All modern bridges interest me for the same reason that spider-webs interest me—the beautiful combination of delicacy and strength.

Bridges also interest me because I find in them the best examples of the fact that when they are efficiently designed for their function they are invariably beautiful, without the separate consideration of Beauty being imposed upon them.

□

I find myself unable to believe in Progress—Change, yes. Greater refinements in the methods of destroying Life are the antithesis of Progress.

Where is the increase in spirituality to be found?

The gap between Heaven and Earth widens rather than diminishes. It is easy to believe, looking out of the car window, that we are going somewhere fast when it may be only the landscape is moving. We too readily take for granted one of the great gifts bestowed upon us—our eyes. We seldom use both of them. What are we saving the other one for when they were designed as a pair?

I only know of two instances where use of one eye is adequate for the occasion—looking through a camera at a given subject and looking down a rifle barrel at the target. Both one and the same in principle.

□

Midwest

The subject of Midwest was found in Wisconsin, but that is neither here no there since locale does not play a determining factor in my pictures. My paintings have always been based upon something seen in Nature and that for me is a spring-board from which to take off.

In recent years I became conscious of a fact which prevails with any of us, but generally in the realm of the unconscious.

When we look at any object in Nature we inevitably carry over a memory of the object we have just previously seen.

Since then I have endeavored to combine the memory and the present in a given painting.

Of this intention, Midwest is a representative example.

□

The Problem of the Artist
(For *Christian Science Monitor*)

The problem of the artist is timeless. It is for him to find his relation to the world he lives in and to strive to find expression of that relationship as a means of communication with others.

This will always be true, from the time of Cave Paintings to the day after tomorrow.

EXHIBITIONS AND RELATED REFERENCES

All known one-man exhibitions of Charles Sheeler's work and limited-group exhibitions in which Sheeler participated are included in the following list. Several of the larger survey exhibitions in which he was represented are also included because circumstances such as date, location, or historical importance of the exhibition are considered pertinent to an appreciation of his professional recognition. Sheeler was a regular participant in the many annual and biennial competitive exhibitions sponsored by major American museums (for example, the Carnegie International, Art Institute of Chicago Annual, Corcoran Biennial). These are not included here because their frequency would encumber the listing.

The references cited after the descriptions of exhibitions relate specifically to those exhibitions.

One-man exhibition of paintings. McClees Gallery, Philadelphia, 16-21 November 1908.

No catalogue known.

International Exhibition of Modern Art. Armory of the 69th Regiment, New York, 17 February-15 March 1913; Art Institute of Chicago, 24 March-15 April 1913; Copley Hall, Boston, 28 April-18 May 1913.

Catalogue.

Brown, Milton; Edward H. Dwight; and Joseph S. Trovato. *1913 Armory Show: 50th Anniversary Exhibition.* New York and Utica, New York: Henry Street Settlement and Munson-Williams-Proctor Institute, 1963. (Sheeler works illustrated, 3.)

Special Exhibition of Modern Art Applied to Decoration by Leading American Artists. Montross Gallery, New York, 28 April-22 May 1915.

Catalogue.

The Forum Exhibition of Modern American Painters. Anderson Galleries, New York, 13-25 March 1916.

Catalogue. Contains statement by each member of the organizing committee and by each of the 16 exhibiting artists. (Sheeler works illustrated, 1.)

Wright, Willard Huntington. "The Forum Exhibition." *Forum,* vol. 55, April 1916, p. 469.

Special Exhibition: Arthur B. Davies, Walt Kuhn, Jules Pascin, Charles Sheeler, Max Weber. Montross Gallery, New York, 13 February-3 March 1917.

Catalogue.

Group exhibition of photographs. Modern Gallery, New York, March 1917.

No catalogue known.

Society of Independent Artists First Annual Exhibition. Grand Central Palace, New York, 10 April-6 May 1917.

Catalogue.

One-man exhibition of photographs. Modern Gallery, New York, 3-15 December 1917.

No catalogue known.

Thirteenth annual exhibition of photographs. John Wanamaker Company, Philadelphia, 1918.

No catalogue known.

Fitz, E. G. "A Few Thoughts on the Wanamaker Exhibition." *The Camera*, vol. 22, no. 4 (April 1918), p. 202.

One-man exhibition of paintings and photographs. De Zayas Gallery, New York, 16-23 February 1920.

No catalogue known.

McBride, Henry. "The Work of Charles Sheeler Attracts Attention—Other Exhibitions." *The Sun and New York Herald*, 22 February 1920, sec. 3, p. 7.

One-man exhibition of paintings, drawings, and photographs. Daniel Gallery, New York, April 1922.

No catalogue known.

Group exhibition of paintings. Durand-Ruel Galleries, Paris, November 1923; Whitney Studio Galleries, New York, January 1924.

No catalogue known.

Watson, Forbes. "Opening the New Year . . . The Whitney Studio Galleries." *The Arts*, vol. 5, no. 1 (January 1924), pp. 42, 47, 50-52. (Sheeler works illustrated, 3.)

Exhibition of Selected Works by Charles Sheeler. Whitney Studio Galleries, New York, 1-31 March 1924.

Catalogue.

Watson, Forbes. "Comment . . . The Whitney Galleries." *The Arts*, vol. 5, no. 3 (March 1924), p. 169.

Tri-national group exhibition, directed by Marius De Zayas, under the patronage of Mrs. E. H. Harriman. Durand-Ruel Galleries, Paris, 28 May-25 June 1925; Chenil Galleries, London, October 1925; Wildenstein & Co., New York, 26 January-15 February 1926.

Catalogue not located.

"Paris Postscripts." *The Arts*, vol. 8, no. 1 (July 1925), pp. 51-54. (Sheeler works illustrated, 1.)

Two-man exhibition with Lozowick of paintings. J. B. Neumann's Print Room, New York, 18 January-4 February 1926.

No catalogue known.

Goodrich, Lloyd. "New York Exhibitions: Sheeler and Lozowick." *The Arts*, vol. 9, no. 2 (February 1926), pp. 97, 102-103.

One-man exhibition of photographs. Art Center, New York, February 1926.

No catalogue known.

Film und Foto. International traveling exhibition organized by the Deutschen Werkbundes, initial showing in Stuttgart, summer 1929.

Catalogue for Berlin showing, 19 October-17 November 1929. Contains "Introduction" by Wolfgang Hermann and essay titled "America and Photography" by Edward Wenstorn [Weston].

One-man exhibition of paintings and drawings. The Downtown Gallery, New York, 18 November-7 December 1931.

Catalogue not located.

"Exhibitions in New York: Charles Sheeler, Downtown Gallery." *The Art News,* vol. 30, no. 8 (21 November 1931), pp. 6, 8. (Sheeler works illustrated, 1.)

H. V. D. "Art: Charles Sheeler's Exhibition." *The New York Times,* 19 November 1931, p. 32.

McBride, Henry(?). "Paintings by Charles Sheeler." *The New York Sun,* 21 November 1931, sporting section, p. 12.

Paintings and Drawings by Charles Sheeler. The Arts Club of Chicago, 19 January-2 February 1932.

Catalogue. (Sheeler works illustrated, 1.)

Murals by American Painters and Photographers. Museum of Modern Art, New York, 4 May-1 August 1932.

Catalogue. Contains essays by Lincoln Kirstein and Julien Levy. (Sheeler works illustrated, 1.)

XIX Esposizione Biennale Internazionale d'Arte. Venice, 12 May-12 October 1934.

Catalogue. The American section (2nd ed., pp. 328-338) contains an introduction by Juliana Force.

Watercolors and Drawings by Hopper, Sheeler and Burchfield. Fogg Art Museum, Cambridge, Massachusetts, 5-31 December 1934.

No catalogue.

An Exhibition of Paintings by Charles Birchfield and Charles Sheeler. Society of Arts and Crafts, Detroit, 16 January-2 February 1935.

Catalogue.

Trois Siècles d'Art aux Etats-Unis. Painting, sculpture, architecture, cinema; organized in collaboration with the Museum of Modern Art, New York. Musée du Jeu de Paume, Paris, May-July 1938.

Catalogue. (Sheeler works illustrated, 1.)

Charles Sheeler: Paintings, Drawings, Photographs. The Museum of Modern Art, New York, 4 October-1 November 1939.

Catalogue. Contains "Introduction" by William Carlos Williams and "A Brief Note on the Exhibition" by Charles Sheeler. (Sheeler works illustrated, 30).

Coates, Robert M. "The Art Galleries—A Sheeler Retrospective." *The New Yorker,* vol. 15, no. 35 (14 October 1939), p. 56.

Cortissoz, Royal. "Types American, British and French." *New York Herald Tribune,* 8 October 1939, sec. 6, p. 8.

Crowninshield, Frank. "Charles Sheeler's 'Americana.'" *Vogue,* 15 October 1939, pp. 65, 106. (Sheeler works illustrated, 1.)

Devree, Howard. "Exhibition Reviews: Charles Sheeler Complete." *Magazine of Art,* vol. 32, no. 11 (November 1939), pp. 644-645. (Sheeler works illustrated, 2.)

Genauer, Emily. "Charles Sheeler in One-Man Show." *New York World Telegram,* 7 October 1939, p. 34.

Jewell, Edward Alden. "Sheeler in Retrospect." *The New York Times,* 8 October 1939, sec. 9, p. 9.

Lane, James W. "Of Sheeler's Immaculatism: The Modern Museum's One-Man Show." *The Art News,* vol. 38, no. 1 (7 October 1939), pp. 5-6. (Sheeler works illustrated, 2.)

Charles Sheeler: Power. Six Original Paintings Commissioned for Reproduction in the December 1940 Issue of Fortune. The Downtown Gallery, New York, 2-21 December 1940.

Catalogue. (Sheeler works illustrated, 1.)

J. L. "Sheeler's Symbols of the Machine Age." *The Art News,* vol. 39, no. 10 (7 December 1940), p. 11. (Sheeler works illustrated, 1).

"Power: A Portfolio by Charles Sheeler." *Fortune,* vol. 22, no. 6 (December 1940), pp. 73-83. (Sheeler works illustrated, 6.)

"Sheeler Paints Power." *The Art Digest,* vol. 15, no. 5 (1 December 1940), p. 8. (Sheeler works illustrated, 1.)

A New Realism: Crawford, Demuth, Sheeler, Spencer. Cincinnati Modern Art Society, Cincinnati Art Museum, 12 March-7 April 1941.

Catalogue. Contains "Introduction" by Elizabeth Sacartoff. (Sheeler works illustrated, 1.)

Paintings by Charles Sheeler. The Dayton [Ohio] Art Institute, 1-30 November 1944.

No catalogue.

Exhibition of Recent Paintings by Charles Sheeler. The Downtown Gallery, New York, 5-23 March 1946.

Catalogue. (Sheeler works illustrated, 1.)

McBride, Henry. "Asceticism Pays: The Art of Charles Sheeler Now Has a Definite Following." *The New York Sun,* 9 March 1946.

"Sheeler—1946." *Art News,* vol. 45, no. 1 (March 1946), pp. 30-31. (Sheeler works illustrated, 3.)

Charles Sheeler: Paintings, Drawings and Photographs. Addison Gallery of American Art, Andover, Massachusetts, 25 October-25 November 1946.

No catalogue.

5 Prodigal Sons: Crawford, Davis, Demuth, Levi, Sheeler. Coleman Art Gallery, Philadelphia, 1947.

Catalogue not located.

Charles Sheeler. The Currier Gallery of Art, Manchester, New Hampshire, 4 January-2 Febuary 1948.

Catalogue.

Charles Sheeler. The Downtown Gallery, New York, 25 January-12 February 1949.

Catalogue.

Preston, Stuart. "5 Stars for February . . . Sheeler." *Art News,* vol. 47, no. 10 (February 1949), pp. 15-16. (Sheeler works illustrated, 1.)

Sheeler [and] Dove: Exhibition. Contemporary Arts Museum, Houston, 7-23 January 1951.

Catalogue. Contains statement by Edith Gregor Halpert.

Paintings, 1949 to 1951, by Charles Sheeler. The Downtown Gallery, New York, 13-31 March 1951.

Catalogue.

Charles Sheeler. Walker Art Center, Minneapolis, 18 May-15 June 1952.

No catalogue.

Ben Shahn, Charles Sheeler, Joe Jones. The Detroit Institute of Arts, 9 March-11 April 1954.

Catalogue. Contains "Introduction" by E. P. Richardson.

Charles Sheeler: A Retrospective Exhibition. Art Galleries, University of California at Los Angeles, October 1954. Tour: M. H. De Young Memorial Museum, San Francisco; Fort Worth Art Center; Munson-Williams-Proctor Institute, Utica, New York; Pennsylvania Academy of the Fine Arts, Philadelphia; San Diego Fine Arts Gallery.

Catalogue. Contains "Foreword" by William Carlos Williams and essays: "An Appreciation," by Bartlett H. Hayes, Jr., and "Charles Sheeler," by Frederick S. Wight. (Sheeler works illustrated, 29.)

Art in America, vol. 42, October 1954, pp. 180-215. (Duplicates text section of catalogue.)

Chanin, A. L. "Charles Sheeler: Purist Brush and Camera Eye." *Art News,* vol. 54, no. 4 (summer 1955), pp. 40-41, 70-72. (Sheeler works illustrated, 4.)

Arthur Dove [and] Charles Sheeler. Hilson Gallery, Deerfield Academy, Deerfield, Massachusetts, 12 February-11 March 1956.

No catalogue.

Sheeler: From the Collection of the William H. Lane Foundation. The Downtown Gallery, New York, 3-28 April 1956.

Catalogue. (Sheeler works illustrated, 1.)

Coates, Robert M. "Art Galleries: Exhibition at Downtown Gallery." *The New Yorker,* vol. 32, 14 April 1956, p. 112.

Sheeler: Recent Paintings. The Downtown Gallery, New York, 25 March-19 April 1958.

Catalogue. (Sheeler works illustrated, 2.)

Charles Sheeler: A Retrospective Exhibition from the William H. Lane Foundation. The New Gallery, Charles Hayden Memorial Library, Massachusetts Institute of Technology, Cambridge, 5 January-22 February 1959.

Catalogue. Contains essay by William Carlos Williams titled "Sheeler—An Appraisal," which is a reprint of "Foreword" in catalogue of 1954 exhibition at University of California, Los Angeles. (Sheeler works illustrated, 4.)

The Precisionist View in American Art. Walker Art Center, Minneapolis, 13 November-25 December 1960. Tour: Whitney Museum of American Art, New York; Detroit Institute of Arts; Los Angeles County Museum, Los Angeles; San Francisco Museum of Art.

Catalogue. Contains essay by Martin L. Friedman. (Sheeler works illustrated, 8.)

Kramer, Hilton. "The American Precisionists." *Arts,* vol. 35, no. 6 (March 1961), pp. 32-37. (Sheeler works illustrated, 2.)

Charles Sheeler: Retrospective Exhibition. Allentown [Pennsylvania] Art Museum, 17 November-31 December 1961.

Catalogue. Contains "Introduction" by Richard Hirsch. (Sheeler works illustrated, 7.)

The Quest of Charles Sheeler: 83 Works Honoring His 80th Year. The University of Iowa, Iowa City, 17 March-14 April 1963.

Catalogue. Contains essay on "Charles Sheeler" by Lillian Dochterman. (Sheeler works illustrated, 29.)

Charles Sheeler: Exhibition, Tempera on Plexiglass. The Downtown Gallery, New York, 4-23 January 1965.

Catalogue. (Sheeler works illustrated, 1.)

Sheeler (1883-1965). The Downtown Gallery, New York, 3-27 May 1966.

Catalogue. (Sheeler works illustrated, 2.)

Charles Sheeler: A Retrospective Exhibition. Cedar Rapids [Iowa] Art Center, 25 October-26 November 1967.

Catalogue. Contains essay titled "Charles Sheeler: The Evolution of a Personal Style," by Donn L. Young. (Sheeler works illustrated, 9.)

SELECTED REFERENCES

American Art Portfolio, Series One. New York: Raymond and Raymond, 1936.

Ames, Winslow. "A Portrait of American Industry." *Worcester* [Massachusetts] *Art Museum Annual,* vol. 2, 1936-1937, pp. 96-98. (Sheeler works illustrated, 1.)

Andrews, Faith, and Edward D. Andrews. "Sheeler and the Shakers." *Art in America,* vol. 53, no. 1 (February 1965), pp. 90-95. (Sheeler works illustrated, 10.)

[Material on Charles Sheeler at] Archives of American Art: Transcripts of recorded interviews with Sheeler by Bartlett Cowdrey (9 December 1958) and Martin Friedman (18 June 1959); microfilm (NSh1, 521 frames) including "The Black Book," manuscript autobiography, photographs, correspondence, scrapbook of press clippings. Detroit and New York.

Baur, John I. H. "A 'Classical' Modern." *The Brooklyn Museum Quarterly,* vol. 26, no. 1 (January 1939), pp. 23-24.

Brace, Ernest. "Charles Sheeler." *Creative Art,* vol. 11, no. 2 (October 1932), pp. 96-104. (Sheeler works illustrated, 7.)

Broom, vol. 5, no. 3 (October 1923), illustrations opposite pp. 129, 144, 160, 161, 176, 177.

Brown, Milton W. *American Painting from the Armory Show to the Depression.* Princeton University Press, 1955. (Sheeler works illustrated, 5.)

"Charles Sheeler." *Index of Twentieth Century Artists,* vol. 3, no. 4 (January 1936), pp. 229-231; supplement.

"Charles Sheeler, Painter, 81, Dead." *The New York Times,* 8 May 1965, p. 8.

Cohen, George Michael. "Charles Sheeler." *American Artist,* vol. 23, no. 1 (January 1959), pp. 32-37, 66-68. (Sheeler works illustrated, 13.)

Coke, Van Deren. *The Painter and The Photographer* (exhibition catalogue). Albuquerque: The University of New Mexico Press, 1964. (Sheeler works illustrated, 2.)

Craven, George M. "Sheeler at Seventy-Five." *College Art Journal,* vol. 18, no. 2 (winter 1959), pp. 136-143. (Sheeler works illustrated, 7.)

Craven, Thomas. "Charles Sheeler." *Shadowland,* vol. 8, no. 1 (March 1923), pp. 10-11, 71. (Sheeler works illustrated, 1.)

Froman, Robert. "Charles Sheeler: 'Super-Realist' with a Paintbrush." *Pageant,* vol. 3, no. 5 (June 1947), pp. 65-73. (Sheeler works illustrated, 7.)

Hare, Susanna, and Edith Porada. *The Great King, King of Assyria: Assyrian Reliefs in the Metropolitan Museum of Art Photographed by Charles Sheeler.* New York: Metropolitan Museum of Art, 1945.

[Kellogg, Florence Loeb.] F. L. K. "Order in the Machine Age." *The Survey,* vol. 67, no. 11 (1 March 1932), pp. 589-591. (Sheeler works illustrated, 3.)

Kootz, Samuel M. "Ford Plant Photos of Charles Sheeler." *Creative Art,* vol. 8, no. 4 (April 1931), pp. 246-267. (Sheeler works illustrated, 3.)

________. *Modern American Painters.* New York: Brewer and Warren, 1930. (Sheeler works illustrated, 4.)

[McCoy, Garnett.] G. McC. "Charles Sheeler: Some Early Documents and a Reminiscence." *Journal of the Archives of American Art,* vol. 5, no. 2 (April 1965), pp. 1-4.

Millard, Charles W. "Charles Sheeler: American Photographer." *Contemporary Photographer,* vol. 6, no. 1 (1968). (Sheeler works illustrated, 41.)

Parker, Robert Allerton. "The Classical Vision of Charles Sheeler." *International Studio,* vol. 84, May 1926, pp. 68-72. (Sheeler works illustrated, 3.)

Richardson, Edgar P. "Three American Painters: Sheeler, Hopper, Burchfield." *Perspectives USA,* no. 16, summer 1956, pp. 111-119. (Sheeler works illustrated, 3.)

Rourke, Constance. *Charles Sheeler: Artist in the American Tradition.* New York: Harcourt, Brace, 1938. (Sheeler works illustrated, 48.)

Scott, Nora [text], and Charles Sheeler [photographs]. *Egyptian Statues.* New York: Metropolitan Museum of Art, 1945.

________. *Egyptian Statuettes.* New York: Metropolitan Museum of Art, 1946.

Sheeler, Charles. "Notes on an Exhibition of Greek Art." *The Arts,* vol. 7, no. 3 (March 1925), p. 153.

________. "Recent Photography by Alfred Stieglitz." *The Arts,* vol. 3, no. 5 (May 1923), p. 345.

"Sheeler Finds Beauty in the Commonplace." *Life,* vol. 5, no. 6 (8 August 1938), pp. 42-45. (Sheeler works illustrated, 5.)

Watson, Forbes. "Charles Sheeler." *The Arts,* vol. 3, no. 5 (May 1923), pp. 335-344. (Sheeler works illustrated, 12.)

________. "New Books on Art: In the American Tradition." *Magazine of Art,* vol. 31, no. 1 (October 1938), pp. 600-608. (Sheeler works illustrated, 1.)

Whelan, Anne. "Barn Is Thing of Beauty to Charles Sheeler, Artist." *The Bridgeport* [Connecticut] *Sunday Post,* 21 August 1938, sec. B, p. 4.

Wight, Frederick S. "Charles Sheeler." In, John I. H. Baur [ed.], *New Art in America: Fifty Painters of the 20th Century.* Greenwich, Connecticut: New York Graphic Society in cooperation with Frederick A. Praeger, Inc., 1957.

1 Plums on a Plate circa 1910

2 Landscape with Waterfall 1911

3 Chrysanthemums 1912

5 The Mandarin 1912

4 Dahlias and Asters 1912

6 Still Life, Spanish Shawl 1912

7 Landscape 1913

18 Flower in Bowl 1918

9 House with Trees 1915

19 Bucks County Barn 1918

27 Offices 1922

23 New York 1920

26 Still Life circa 1922

29 Geraniums, Pots, Spaces 1923

34 Apples 1924

33 Objects on a Table 1924

35 Timothy 1924

42 Pennsylvania Landscape 1925

39 Gladioli in White Pitcher 1925

41 Landscape—Truro 1925

44 Geranium circa 1926

45 Interior 1926

47 Spring Interior 1927

48 Delmonico Building 1927

53 Rouge River Industrial Plant 1928

65 View of Central Park 1932

64 Ballet Mechanique 1931

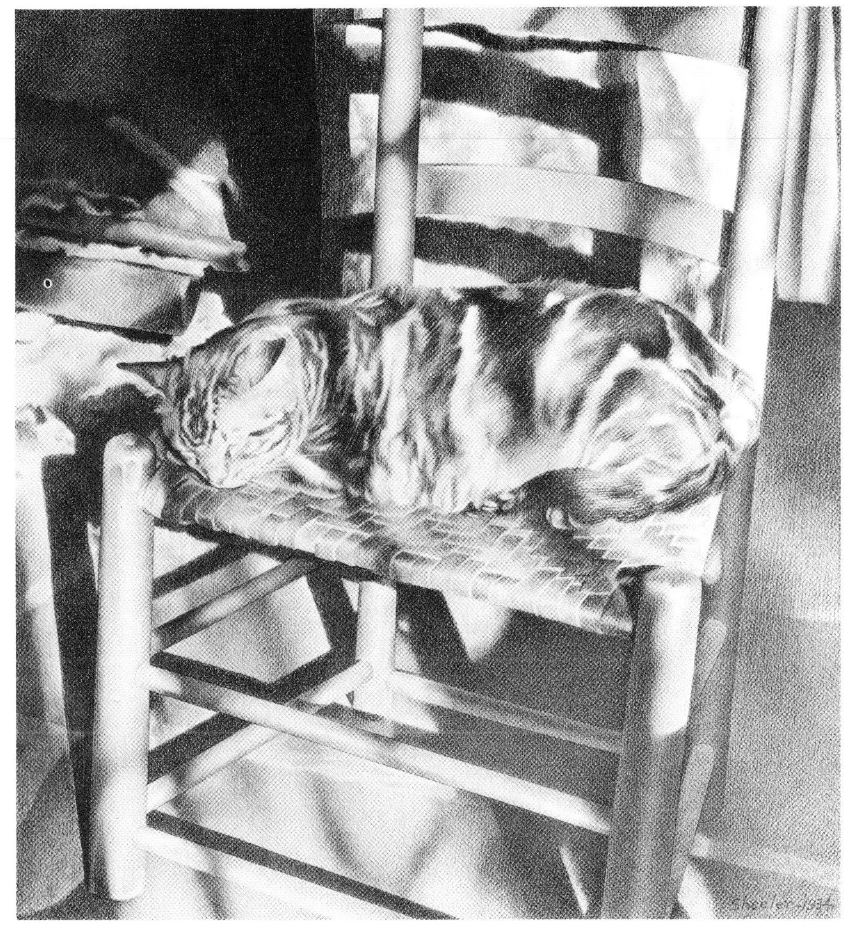

71 Feline Felicity 1934

66 New Haven 1932

69 Bucks County Barn 1932

72 American Interior 1934

73 Ephrata 1934

74 · Shaker Buildings 1934

80 Totems in Steel 1935

87 Silo 1938

82 Rocks at Steichen's 1937

93 Shaker Detail 1941

94 Red against the Light 1942

92 Neighbors 1940

101 Fissures 1945

102 Fugue 1945

103 Water 1945

108 Classic Still Life 1947

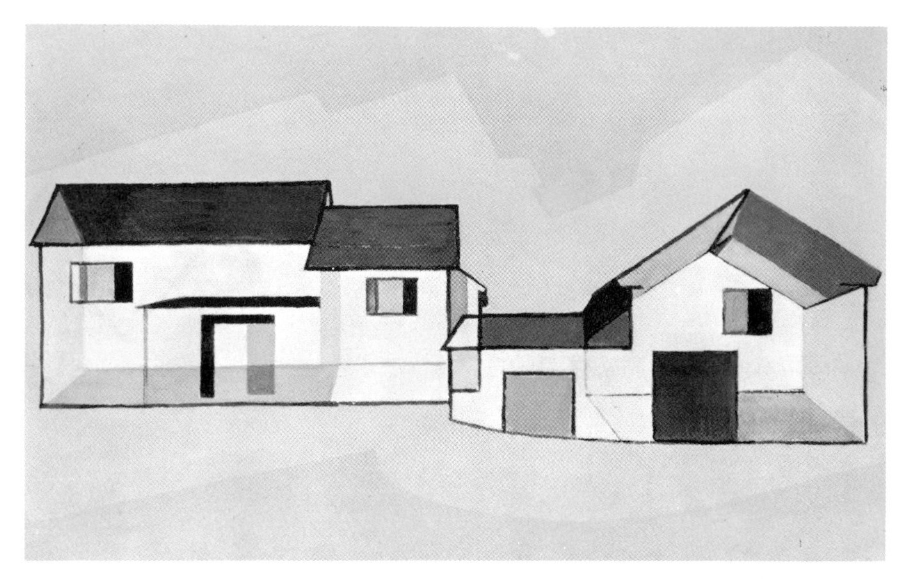

110 On the Theme of Farm Buildings #2 1947

104 The Yellow Wall 1946

115 Amoskeag Mills 1948

119 Variations in Red 1949

116 Buildings at Lebanon 1949

131 New York #2 1951

121 Improvisations on a Mill Town 1949

127 Skyline 1950

123 Family Group 1950

133 Conversation Piece 1952

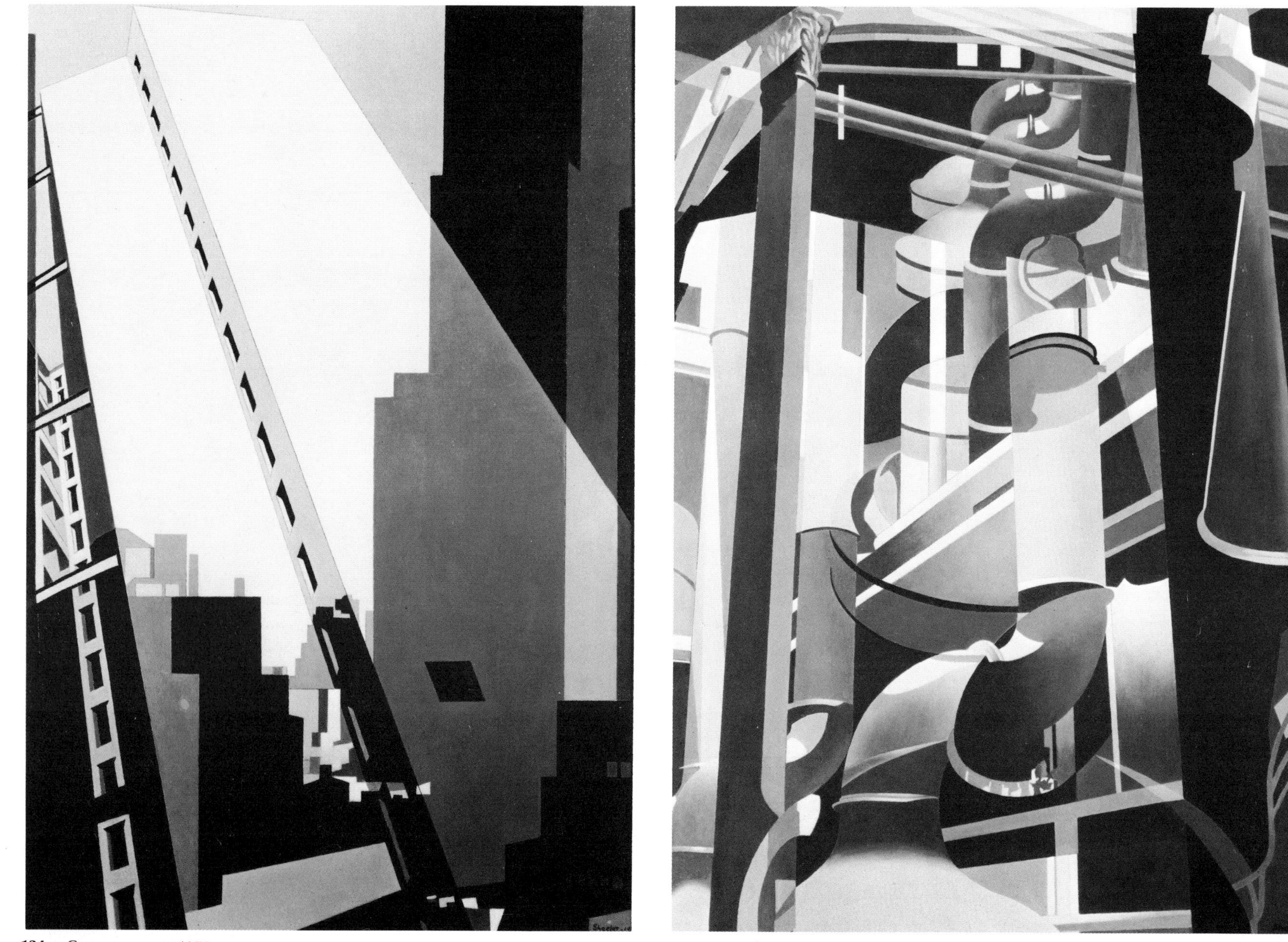

134 Convergence 1952

136 Convolutions 1952

142 Steel—Croton 1953

146 Stacks in Celebration 1954

147 Begonias 1955

144 Lunenburg 1954

151 General Motors Research 1955

149 The Web 1955

150 Western Industrial 1955

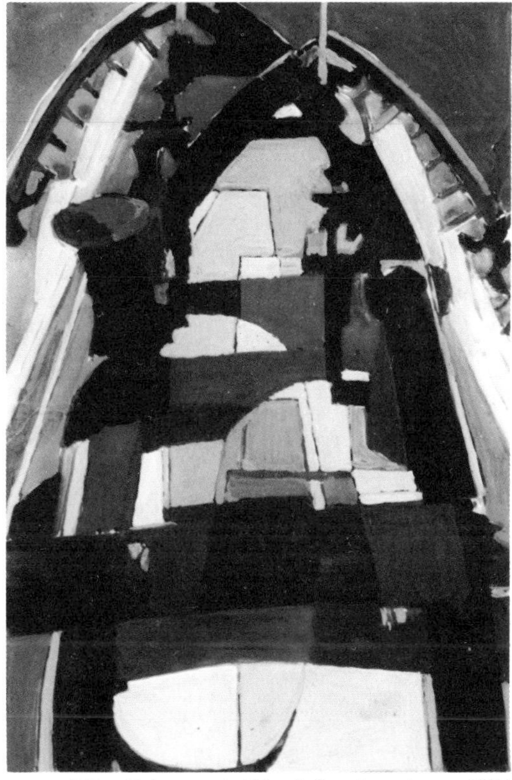
154 Fisherman's Wharf, San Francisco 1956

155 San Francisco 1956

156 The Great Tree 1957

158 Yosemite #2 1957

157 The Great Tree 1957

169 Sun, Rocks, and Trees 1959

159 Two against the White 1957

163 Continuity 1957

161 Red against the White 1957

164 Continuity #2 1957

162 California Industrial 1957

8 Zinnia and Nasturtium Leaves 1915

21 New York 1920

22 New York 1920

17 African Figures 1917

46 Portrait circa 1926

49 River Rouge Plant—Power House 1927

51 River Rouge Plant—Stamping Press 1927

56 Chartres Cathedral 1929

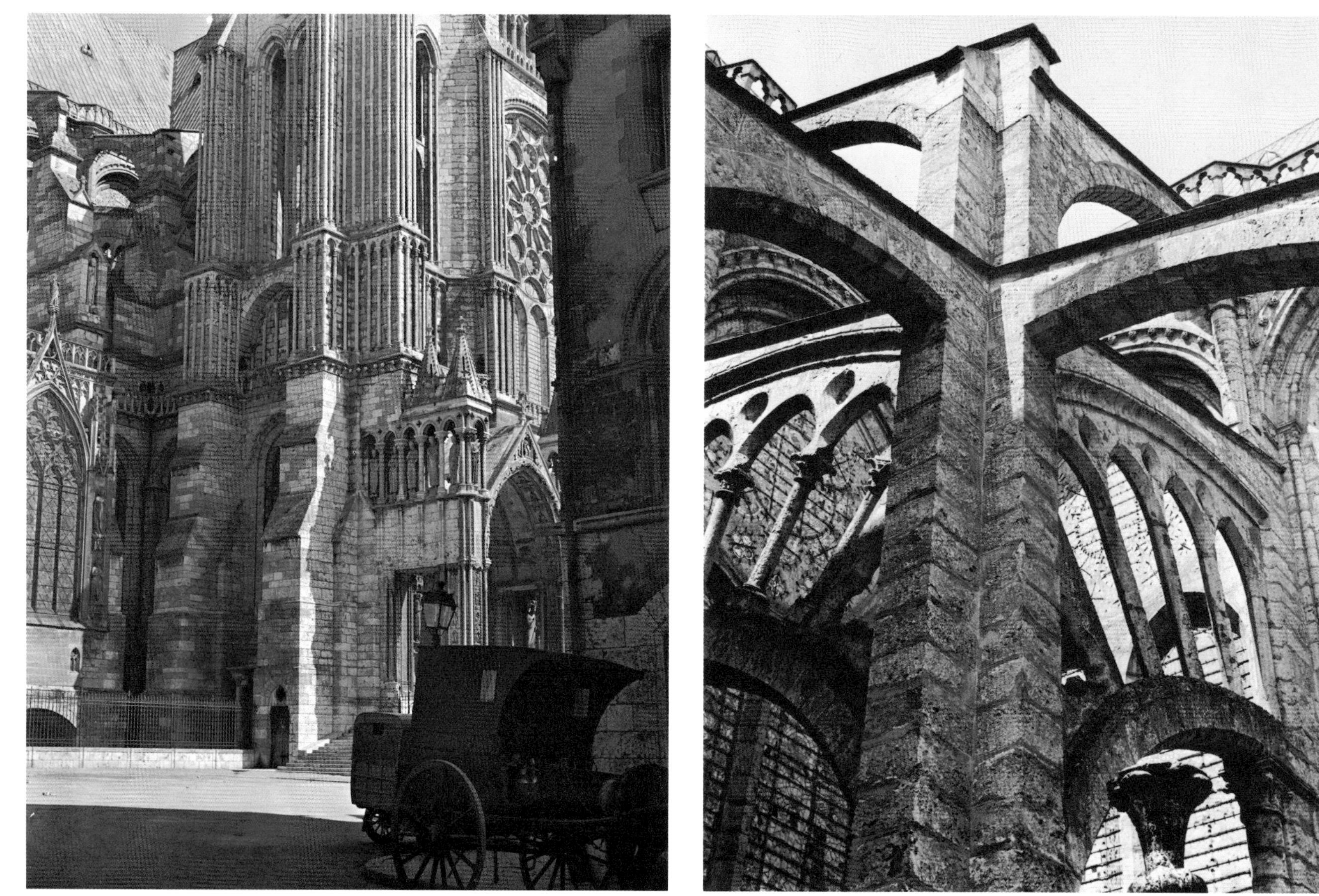

57 Chartres Cathedral 1929

58 Chartres Cathedral 1929

76 Coleus 1925

78 Shaker Window circa 1935

85 Portrait circa 1937

84 Clouds 1937

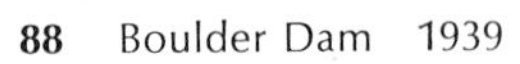

88 Boulder Dam 1939

97 Assyrian Relief 1942

52 Funnel 1927

99 Bust of Andrew Jackson 1943

132 United Nations Building 1951

130 Beech Tree 1951

143 Sequoia 1954

137 Frosted Window circa 1953

INDEX TO REPRODUCTIONS

page no.	catalogue no.	title and date of work
22	91.	Steam Turbine, 1939
129	92.	Neighbors, 1940
128	93.	Shaker Detail, 1941
129	94.	Red against the Light, 1942
22	95.	White Sentinels, 1942
87	96.	Assyrian Relief, 1942
152	97.	Assyrian Relief, 1942
67	98.	The Artist Looks at Nature, 1943
153	99.	Bust of Andrew Jackson, 1943
	100.	Power House with Trees, 1944, *not reproduced*
129	101.	Fissures, 1945
130	102.	Fugue, 1945
131	103.	Water, 1945
132	104.	The Yellow Wall, 1946
48	105.	Incantation, 1946
58	106.	Ballardvale, 1946 (color)
59	107.	Reflection, 1946
131	108.	Classic Still Life, 1947
	109.	Barn Abstraction, 1947, *not reproduced*
131	110.	On the Theme of Farm Buildings #2, 1947
75	111.	Architectural Planes, 1947
	112.	Catwalk, 1947, *not reproduced*
	113.	Thunder Shower, 1948, *not reproduced*
78	114.	Amoskeag Canal, 1948
132	115.	Amoskeag Mills, 1948
134	116.	Buildings at Lebanon, 1949
77	117.	Manchester, 1949
74	118.	Counterpoint, 1949
133	119.	Variations in Red, 1949
72	120.	Ballardvale Revisited, 1929
136	121.	Improvisations on a Mill Town, 1949
66	122.	Wings, 1949
136	123.	Family Group, 1950
	124.	Companions, 1950, *not reproduced*
	125.	New York, 1950, *not reproduced*
88	126.	RCA Building, 1950
136	127.	Skyline, 1950
26	128.	Skyline, 1950
88	129.	Beech Tree, 1951
154	130.	Beech Tree, 1951
135	131.	New York #2, 1951
153	132.	United Nations Building, 1951
137	133.	Conversation Piece, 1952
138	134.	Convergence, 1952
89	135.	Tanks at Cedarburg, 1952
138	136.	Convolutions, 1952
154	137.	Frosted Window, circa 1953
89	138.	Lever Building, 1953
79	139.	New England Irrelevancies, 1953
61	140.	Ore into Iron, 1953
54	141.	Aerial Gyrations, 1953
139	142.	Steel—Croton, 1953
154	143.	Sequoia, 1954
140	144.	Lunenburg, 1954
53	145.	Architectural Cadences, 1954
139	146.	Stacks in Celebration, 1954
139	147.	Begonias, 1955
28	148.	Golden Gate, 1955
141	149.	The Web, 1955
142	150.	Western Industrial, 1955
141	151.	General Motors Research, 1955
	152.	Marin's Rocks, 1956, *not reproduced*
55	153.	On a Shaker Theme, 1956
143	154.	Fisherman's Wharf, San Francisco, 1956
143	155.	San Francisco, 1956
144	156.	The Great Tree, 1957
144	157.	The Great Tree, 1957
144	158.	Yosemite #2, 1957
145	159.	Two against the White, 1957
90	160.	Two against the White, 1957 (color)
145	161.	Red against the White, 1957
146	162.	California Industrial, 1957
145	163.	Continuity, 1957
145	164.	Continuity #2, 1957
62	165.	Continuity, 1957
	166.	On a Connecticut Theme, 1958, *not reproduced*
	167.	Composition around Red (Pennsylvania), 1958, *not reproduced*
31	168.	Hex Signs, 1958
144	169.	Sun, Rocks, and Trees, 1959
65	170.	Composition around White, 1959